DOWRY
OF A
NOBODY

flea market style

flea market style

Emily Chalmers   *with words by Ali Hanan*

photography by Debi Treloar

RYLAND
PETERS
& SMALL

LONDON NEW YORK

First published in
the USA in 2005 by
Ryland Peters & Small, Inc.
519 Broadway
5th Floor
New York, NY 10012
www.rylandpeters.com

10 9 8 7 6 5 4 3

ISBN 10: 1-84172-938-8
ISBN 13: 978-1-84172-938-1

Printed and bound in China.

Library of Congress Cataloging-in-Publication Data
Chalmers, Emily.
  Flea market style / Emily Chalmers ; with words by Ali
Hanan ; photography by Debi Treloar.
     p. cm.
  Includes index.
  ISBN 1-84172-938-8
  1. House furnishings. 2. Interior decoration. 3. Flea
markets. I. Hanan, Ali. II. Title.
  TX311.C43 2005
  747--dc22
                              2005009252

contents

introduction

Imagine. It's a Saturday morning. Rather than heading to the mall, you have strolled to a local market. Each booth brims with gems. In among the bric-à-brac are vintage fabrics, polished silver, fine bone-china teacups, and look!— there's a diamond— a nut-brown leather club chair complete with its original soft velvet cushion.

Sigh. If only your wicker shopping bag were a hundred times larger and came with wheels and an engine. Mall buys pale beside secondhand pieces with colorful past lives. What's more, market pieces survive because they were built for years of service. Old-timers such as copper pots, heirloom linens, mahogany rolltop desks, and cast-iron kettles have done their time— and lived to tell the tale. Some finds were also

created with an artistry increasingly rare and precious in an age of mass-production. The tiny errant line on a hand-painted roll of wallpaper or a thumb print on a handmade vase gives these pieces a twist of humanity.

Beautiful things never go out of style. Classics endure. And, if it's your lucky day, you may even bag a real jewel, like an original Eames chair or a swooping Castiglioni "Swan" lamp, which you can snap up for a song. Pieces like this retain—and even increase—their value.

Some pieces will be welcomed as they are, but others will need tender loving care or urgent cosmetic surgery. Choose a piece if it has promise. If a sofa with good bone structure needs a facelift, for example, simply fashion a cover for it out of a vintage fabric. Other pieces can be resuscitated and reinvented. Dress up a Cinderella pillow with an antique brooch or give a Plain Jane lampshade a gorgeous new gown made from old ribbons. Once you are a seasoned talent scout, you will be able to see a piece's potential and dream up a whole new career for it, like using a bench as a side table or a chipped teacup as a dainty vase.

Dip into the first part of the book, Flea Market Finds, to see what can be on offer at secondhand booths. Whether your style is retro, minimalist, rock-'n'-roll, or eclectic, you will see how to choose furniture, kitchenware, lighting, and fabrics to suit it. Putting It All Together shows you how to transform your interior, room by room. The book ends with ideas on where to source finds. Apart from markets, items are also commonly spotted at garage sales, village fairs, and auctions, in dumpsters and on internet sites.

Be inspired. Turn the pages and discover what kind of orphaned finds you can adopt and bring home to a new life. Shun the consumerism of the chains. Recycle and revive pieces with soul and style—and you will be able to create a loved, lived-in space that you can really call home.

flea market finds

Old chairs, tables, beds, bookcases, desks, drawers, sofas, armchairs, stools, and armoires come in all shapes, sizes, and styles—and can often be picked up for a song. Choose pieces to suit your taste— or create your own eclectic look.

furniture

A home furnished with secondhand pieces seems more lived-in and loved than one furnished mainly with new items. Unlike hot-off-the-shop-floor chain-store products, secondhand things have a casual, careworn air. Some found objects have their own quirks; some need a bit of mending—but give any item a little tender loving care or a fresh twist and watch it blossom into new life.

What's more, market-found furniture comes in an enormous range of decorative styles. Timeless pieces, such as old leather sofas and refectory tables, have an important feature in common with faded denim jeans and little black dresses: they always look good. For urban loft dwellers, there are pieces to suit the raw, hard edges of industrial chic (think old dental chairs, office swivel seats, filing cabinets). For those who hanker after the soft, rustic looks of country style, many markets have whole fields of furniture ripe for harvesting (think wicker storage baskets, wooden rocking chairs, farmhouse-style tables). If your taste is retro, you will find a feast of vintage furniture, including

ABOVE Who would have imagined that this lovely lady in red would need rescuing from a dumpster? She now looks stunning in a vibrant scarf, fashioned into a pillow cover.

OPPOSITE Many once-loved pieces need a simple makeover. For example, a set of drawers that came from an office looks pretty in a coat of pink paint.

Think of yourself as a talent scout seeking supermodels. You will quickly learn how to spot a gorgeous piece at a hundred paces.

wooden sideboards, kidney-shaped tables, and low-level vinyl sofas. Whatever your style, there will always be something to satisfy the magpie instinct.

While you are bound to find something to suit your taste, you will also find classics at affordable prices. Buying brand-new high-quality pieces is very expensive, but if you buy new low-cost furniture, the choice is mainly restricted to flat-packed items, which tend to push a self-destruct button after only a few months of use. If you bone up on design classics, you could unearth a coveted gem such as an original Verner Panton "S" chair or a Charles and Ray Eames recliner. Such treasures will retain or even increase their value if kept in mint condition, so when it comes to reselling them you could be (literally) sitting on a small fortune.

When it comes to buying furniture, think of yourself as a talent scout searching for potential supermodels. You will quickly learn how to spot a gorgeous piece at a hundred paces. Start by checking for sound bone structure and chose one with a sturdy, hardy frame, springs and legs, and intact stuffing. If the piece of furniture is in good shape but looks haggard, think cosmetic surgery. It is easy to give furniture a facelift with a new coat of paint, a new cover, or a little artful customizing. Try furniture out before you buy it, since looks can be deceptive (you don't want a spring sticking into your back when you're reading the Sunday papers).

THIS PAGE Let an old sofa step out in style in a new dress; this one has had its aging white cover dyed a refreshing blue.

OPPOSITE, ABOVE Hallways are frequently no more than traffic routes, but with a hip find such as this retro chair, you won't want to just walk on by.

OPPOSITE, BELOW LEFT A luxurious red leather sofa has had its sassy looks softened by a floral pillow sewn from an old kitchen curtain.

OPPOSITE, BELOW RIGHT This "Swan" chair by Danish designer Arne Jacobsen was discovered at a Copenhagen market.

THIS PAGE An antique, gilt-edged console found at London's Portobello market gives a modern space an air of old-fashioned luxury. Adorning its smooth top is an oriental-style glass tree plucked from a yard sale, now used to display its owner's jewelry. The print above is a common, but classic, art find.

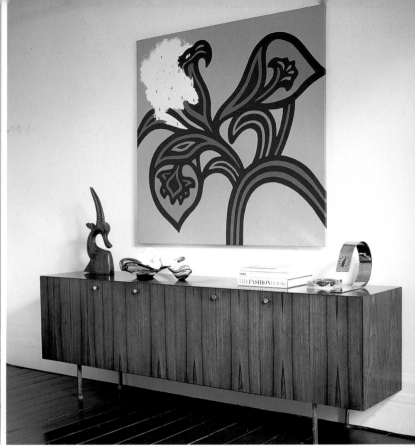

Some found objects have quirks; some need mending—but give any item a little tender loving care or a fresh twist and watch it blossom into new life.

Seating is an essential element of virtually every space in the home, especially the living room. When it comes to armchairs and sofas, watch out for signs of use such as shiny patches on arms or saggy seating. Those details suggest that the seat is comfortable enough to have been sat on for hours in the past. One thing that seems to appeal to all tastes is the come-hither warmth of a loved leather sofa. Other fabric-covered pieces may be found in great shape but with a dated "dress," so re-upholster them in a new or vintage fabric. For an instant new cover, drape an old bedspread, checked

blanket, or faux fur throw over the sofa. Or add *va-va-vroom* with pillows made from vintage fabrics and adorned with brooches, ribbons, or buttons.

While sofas and armchairs are at home in living rooms, so too are pieces like chaises-longues and daybeds. Old chaise-longues often bring with them an air of elegance and grandeur. If quirky modern is your style, make an old-world chaise-longue more funky by re-upholstering it with a zebra print cover; if you're a classicist, complement its antique charm with embroidered silk cushions. These pieces look seductive in a bedroom or decadent in a bathroom.

ABOVE LEFT Bring old pieces into rooms for which they were not originally intended. Repainted crisp white, this chest of drawers is at home in a minimalist-style living room.

ABOVE A sideboard from the 1960s is used for both storage and display. The "paint by numbers" picture above it was inspired by a vintage silk scarf pattern.

therapists' chairs, bar stools, architects' chairs, laboratory stools, and office chairs. Your finds may need a little paintwork here or a new cover there, but they will introduce into your home elements that are slightly eccentric and fabulously original.

You may find it hard to find a complete set of dining chairs, so cherry-pick individual chairs with a common theme (fold-out garden chairs, wooden café chairs, or 1960s chairs) to create harmony —or go eclectic and create an array of mismatching chairs, softening hard edges and giving a sense of "family" with a range of matching cushions.

When it comes to tables, aficionados can choose from secondhand office desks, old garden tables,

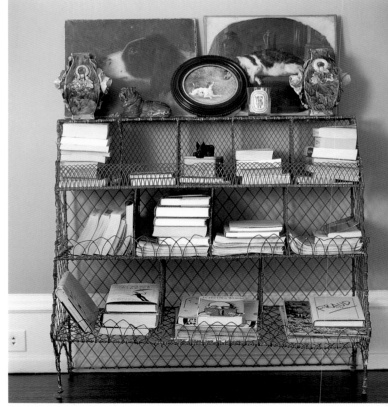

A daybed is easy to make (simply shorten the legs of a small single bed) and is usually handier than a pull-out sofa for overnight guests. Create a backrest of multicolored cushions for daytime use.

Another junk find that's often dismissed is the bench (think old church pews or school-assembly benches). Often made from best-quality wood, a bench can double as a table or as overflow seating for dinner parties. To make it comfortable, simply fashion some squab cushions from vintage fabrics.

The choice of chairs is as endless as the way in which they can be used. Seek out old wrought-iron chairs, ex-café chairs, metal stools, rocking chairs, and wicker chairs for every room, but also think laterally, bringing home retired "working" chairs such as dentists' chairs, old theater seats, massage

THIS PAGE A handsome cabinet with sliding doors offers generous storage for all sorts of recycled boxes housing odds and ends.

OPPOSITE, LEFT A piece of salvaged netting divides this living space into zones. The chair is an electric massage chair; originally clad in vinyl, it has been stripped down and re-upholstered in floral fabrics for a softer look.

OPPOSITE, RIGHT Outdoor pieces can work well indoors; this former wire-mesh plant rack has been reinvented as a shelf for books and ornaments.

THIS PAGE AND OPPOSITE Be inventive, like the owner of this house, who has jazzed up pieces of furniture with a thick coat of blackboard paint. She has chalked her son's name all over his chest of drawers and adorned the hall cupboard with poetry in a flowing, looping hand. These furniture sculptures are thrown into relief by a canvas of pale-gray walls.

THIS PAGE Markets offer many storage pieces such as the chests below (left and right); customize them with brightly hued paints. A set of mirrors in various shapes (below left) does the same job on a wall as a single long mirror.

OPPOSITE Once used to store household linens, this old armoire now houses a collection of dishes. Beside it is a found sofa, which demonstrates how a kitsch, chintzy piece can appear lustrous when set against a plain canvas.

bedside tables, and pine refectory tables. The list is endless. If you have enough space, look for one of the many farmhouse-style pine tables that turn up at furniture markets; if you don't have much space, alternatives include tables with drop leaves or extendable tables to accommodate surplus guests. Then there is always the ultimate junk-find table: a sanded door or a large piece of heavy glass mounted on a pair of reclaimed trestles; just cover it with a beautiful cloth to hide its haphazard look.

You will find many retro kidney tables or bent-chrome-and-glass 1970s tables to serve as coffee tables. As for bedside tables, the choice depends on how inventive you are. Tables big enough for a couple of books, a reading light, and a water glass are easily fashioned out of small wooden stools, old school desks, or folding butler's tray tables.

Wooden tea trolleys make equally useful kitchen storage. Alternatively, you can sever the trolley's legs to make an instant side table or children's dining table. Many former work tables such as office desks, sewing tables, and architects' drawing boards can be converted into home-office desks.

Efficient storage is an essential element of any home. Chests of drawers, side cabinets, armoires, bookcases, plate racks, and cupboards—in all shapes and sizes—turn up regularly at secondhand outlets and in a huge range of styles.

All you need to do to update them is to sand them and give them a fresh, thick coat of paint, or paper the doors with vintage wallpaper. Or you could customize drawers with funky new handles (fashion a handle out of old rope or thick ribbon or use vintage door handles). Old tea chests, beautiful antique leather suitcases, toy chests, big wicker baskets, old laundry baskets, and wine boxes also create covetable storage.

One easy way to introduce pattern, color, and texture into a Cinderella interior is with textiles. Every market or secondhand store is a treasure trove of curtains, quilts, lace, shawls, tea towels, and end-cuts of fabric bolts—in a wide range of weights, qualities, and patterns. Another solution is the clever use of junk–find wallpapers.

pattern and color

OPPOSITE A boldly striped pillow and throw have been used to update an old sofa, whose arms fold down to create a daybed. A patchwork of wallpaper samples adorns the wall behind it.

ABOVE RIGHT Don't judge a chair by its cover. If you like the shape of a chair but not its garb, simply have it re-upholstered.

Observe how easily something ordinary can become extraordinary through the addition of pattern and color from fabrics, wallpapers, or paints. Imagine covering a plain wall with a patchwork of wallpaper samples. Or visualize a minimalist bedroom with a wrought-iron bed covered in a stark white bedcover and an old armoire in the corner. Garnish the bed with one colorful cushion, and somehow the whole room is transformed. It is softer. It has a center. That is the quiet power of pattern and color.

When you use pattern, remember that a little goes a long way. Pattern draws the eye, becoming a focal point, so mix it with plenty of large plain areas. If you want your busy, chintzy sofa to be your living room's exclamation mark, keep the backdrop plain. Conversely, if you have discovered a roll of graphically decorated 1970s wallpaper, make sure the sofa in front of it is neutral.

Color schemes usually work best when devised in one of three ways: by using contrasting colors (for example, red teamed with blue, or turquoise with orange); or by using complementary tones of the same color (for example, khaki, sage, and lime green, or cobalt blue, azure, and sky blue); or by combining harmonious colors (for example, ruby red and orange, or chocolate and violet).

Ideas for decorative schemes have many sources. You could base your color palette on a find such as a roll of vintage floral wallpaper, a beautiful orange vase, or a red leather sofa, or you might prefer to search for accessories once you have chosen your favorite paint color as a backdrop. A fresh green, for example, may prompt you to track down natural or naturally inspired objects to accompany it, such as a nut-brown leather sofa, a wooden-framed mirror, or a large leafy plant in a terracotta pot.

Remember that light colors make small spaces appear bigger, while dark colors make walls feel closer. If you want to alter the way your space is perceived, apply these rules by bringing color, pattern, and texture into the floor and walls—your interior's largest canvases.

ABOVE Stack patterned fabric finds to create small piles of visual interest.

OPPOSITE Just as you might do with an outfit, you can crown your sofa or bed with a chic accessory. Here, a trio of cushions made from vintage scarves turn heads on a bed.

THIS PAGE Soften the hard edges of wooden chairs with cushions. This foursome was created from various floral finds. Being fashioned from fabrics with a related color theme makes them into a set.

LEFT This beautiful fabric length, used as a curtain to inhibit cold drafts, is like an artwork in itself. The hard look of the door, covered in blackboard paint, is instantly softened with a white lace curtain.

RIGHT Held in place by pebbles from the beach, a floral scarf makes a translucent window blind.

Avoid visual mayhem by papering a single wall and painting the room's other walls in a neutral color.

LEFT Use finds to create screens and drapes that dare to be different. This striking patchwork of silk scarves, all loosely tacked together, offsets the hard-edged feel of a former warehouse. An old metal mailroom cabinet is home to piles of fabric finds, all waiting to be used.

Secondhand wall hangings and wallpaper are ideal for revitalizing your space. Unpopular in the 1990s—when white paint splashed its way over countless interior walls—wallpaper is now making a comeback. With it comes color, pattern and, in some cases, texture. Secondhand markets offer a range of vintage papers. Visual mayhem can easily be avoided by papering a single wall and painting the other walls a neutral color. Sometimes you will find insufficient wallpaper to cover the whole wall. If this happens, look for a complementary paper and paper the wall in alternating stripes. Some

wallpaper patterns are overpowering, but, if you are passionate about a particular design or find a beautiful piece of wrapping paper, use it to jazz up other surface areas, such as storage boxes, files, closet doors, headboards, and built-in bathtub exteriors. Old hand-painted papers are sometimes masterpieces in their own right. Turn them into display items by inserting a cutting into a big wooden frame or papering a wrap-around canvas.

When it comes to floors, you will unearth a wealth of coverings at secondhand markets. If you discover a beautiful piece, nothing will show it off

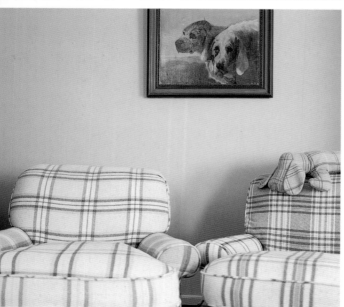

ABOVE Thick wool rugs make hard-wearing chair covers. This old army rug is tacked onto the chair in a big blanket stitch.

ABOVE LEFT Sew squares of handmade antique lace onto plain cushions to give them depth and texture.

LEFT Old Welsh blankets cover a once disheveled pair of armchairs. Out of the blanket remnants a dog was born.

quite like a white or light wood floor. For patterned looks, search for Turkish kilims or Indian dhurries— or, if you find a carpet you like, simply cut off a piece to use as a rug. Heavy quilts can also work on the floor. Animal skins feel sensuously soft underfoot, so hunt down sheepskin, cowhide, goatskin, fake zebra prints, and similar pieces.

Many fabrics found at markets are exceptionally good quality, such as antique linen, classic cotton, thick wool blankets, and handmade lace. Textiles that survive years of servitude do so because they are resilient, and most of them are made of natural fibers. Some pieces may be slightly threadbare, frayed, or bleached out, but these timeworn old dames inject a relaxed, lived-in feel to your home.

RIGHT Antique handmade tablecloths make delicate window covers, allowing light to penetrate through the weave while banishing inquisitive eyes.

BELOW Dress up a chair with cushions made out of little black dresses. Former sequined gowns give this black-linen-covered chair instant glamour.

Like the most durable fabrics, certain prints stand the test of time, including polka dots, stripes (particularly red-white or blue-white stripes), florals, graphic patterns, gingham, animal prints, crochet squares, and paisleys. Patterns from different eras work well together (an Art Deco print and a 1950s print, a 1970s paisley print with a 1930s floral design) and look equally alluring with modern prints. As with paint, you can either mix similar patterns or bring together polka dots, stripes, and graphics for a bold, audacious look. Remember to make the most of pattern with plain. Your eye will

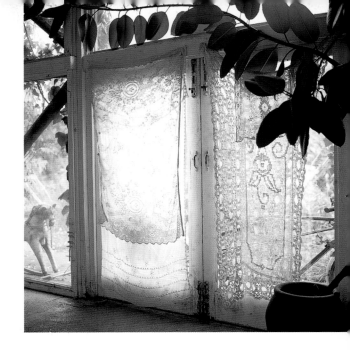

Heavy quilts and animal hides, such as sheepskin, goatskin, and cowhide, make wonderfully soft and sensuous floor coverings.

appreciate a jewellike collection of throw pillows on a fresh, white sofa or a patchwork quilt crowned with white linen pillows.

When looking for secondhand fabrics, start with conventional sources, but don't forget that vintage clothing is also a treasure trove of textiles waiting to be resuscitated. Vintage dresses, particularly those with full skirts, have lots of fabric to recycle. To create felt, buy a heap of old woolen sweaters and put them through a hot wash. You can easily fashion them into cushion covers or use them to create a winter-weight patchwork quilt.

Other pieces to look out for are pashminas and ponchos, which—in the same way that you would casually throw one over your bare shoulders—you

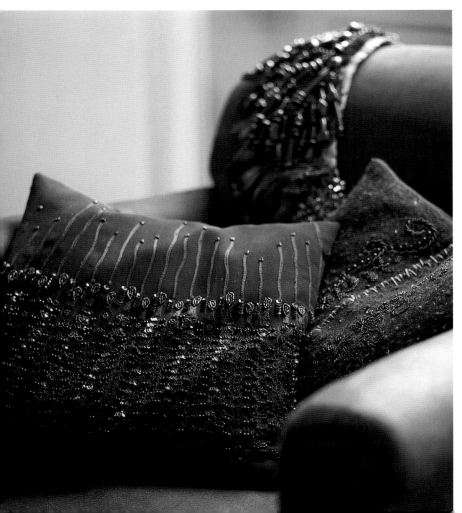

RIGHT To achieve a country feel, combine various types of traditional pattern, such as paisleys, florals, checks, and stripes.

THIS PAGE You might not think that a polka-dot handkerchief, a geometric scarf, a crocheted rug, and two floral cushions would go together, but this artful ensemble is a fine example of effective combining.

OPPOSITE Create your own patchwork quilt from old baby's clothes, vintage dresses, scarves, curtains—whatever you can find. Add a colorful dust ruffle made from an unused tablecloth or fabric roll secured by the weight of the mattress.

LEFT Hide pockmarked tables under unusual tablecloths such as this one, created from the end of a fabric bolt. Antique linen sheets and Indian cotton bedspreads make good washable covers.

RIGHT Vintage tea towels made from robust old linens often surface at markets. Choose ones with funky retro designs.

can drape over sofas and armchairs or sew into cushion covers. Other clothes include silk scarves, which can also be used to make beguiling cushion covers or to adorn plain bedside tables. A black lacy shawl could become a window cover (the light will diffuse through it beautifully). If you have no time for sewing, pay a visit to your local tailor and commission a piece. Pillow covers, for example, are a simple job and shouldn't cost much.

More conventional fabric finds, such as curtains, bedspreads, and tablecloths, will easily find a use in your home. For example, if you possess a large sofa with a drab cover, a vintage bedspread or curtains swathed over the entire piece will hide a multitude of imperfections. Bedspreads, especially old Indian cotton ones, make funky tablecoths and generously large picnic blankets.

Curtains—such as the plush red velvet variety of curtain popular in the 1980s—can also be adapted to make covers for beds or cushions. Designed as an insulating material, luxurious velvet makes a pragmatic winter bedcover. A patchwork quilt could become a striking living-room wall-hanging or a makeshift curtain in a child's room. Every fabric, conventional or otherwise, has endless possibilities.

One of the most rewarding fabrics to keep your eyes open for is antique linen. Once a treasured heirloom, old linen often turns up in markets. It is unbeatable for softness and resilience—consider, for example, freshly ironed linen sheets scented with lavender. If you find an old linen sheet, but parts of it are threadbare, simply cut it up into tea towels. Do as frugal housewives once did and cut down sheets to make handkerchiefs and window-cleaning rags. Old linen tablecloths once came fringed with hand-stitched lace. When hung on a window, these become

You can swathe a vintage bedspread or curtains over a drab sofa to conceal a multitude of imperfections. Bedspreads can also be made into funky tablecloths.

LEFT Introducing fabrics into an interior space has an immediate softening effect, as demonstrated in this room by a brightly colored blanket casually thrown over the arm of a couch. Ethnic rugs of this type were indispensable features of 1960s style— as were flamboyant swirly patterns such as the one seen in the curtain fabric.

perfect blinds, letting in just enough light while at the same time maintaining privacy. In addition to their uses as furnishing accessories, many fabrics can take on more off-beat roles. For an instant artwork, stretch a particularly beautiful piece over an old canvas—or, if you find a dress to die for, model it on a dressmaker's dummy as an instant sculpture.

ABOVE Crochet throws lend a soft, homey feel to several rooms in the home. Sofas, armchairs, daybeds, and beds all love curling up with a crochet blanket.

THIS PAGE From the tarnished silver cup to the antique perfume bottle and the envelope fashioned out of an old music score, these pieces come from a similar palette and share an otherworldly feel—so they work well as a group.

RIGHT Soda siphons in green or clear glass are a common sight at markets.

RIGHT Soda siphons in green or clear glass are a common sight at markets.

BELOW Create your own sparkling floral display out of crystal chandelier drops and artificial flowers made from antique fabric scraps stretched around pliable piping. Arrange with care in a sturdy vase to match.

Ceramics and glass are the jewels of your interior space. Just as one big ruby pendant can transform a little black dress, so can a single red vase add vibrancy and a touch of drama to a slate–colored room.

ceramics and glass

Use ceramics and glass to add glamour and beauty to your home. Imagine, for example, a windowsill adorned with a string of sparkling perfume bottles or a table dressed with a necklace of Moroccan tea glasses with glowing votive lights inside.

Allow yourself to be seduced by stall after stall of shapely bowls, elegant vases and candelabra, handsome earthenware pots, dainty glasses, and pretty plates. There is a multitude of castaways just begging to be rescued and brought home.

Such beautiful vintage finds are very much in vogue. Open any recent interiors magazine and you'll see how desirable previously loved glassware and ceramics have become. Pieces such as delicate, hand-painted teacups, crystal cake stands, and futuristic 1950s vases are selling like hot cakes

ABOVE Ceramic and glass vessels make colorful, elegant containers for everyday kitchen herbs.

RIGHT Unusual flowers bring a born-again quality to secondhand vases.

OPPOSITE, MAIN PICTURE This set of large, sculptural vases had a rather macabre past life as containers for graveyard flowers. Now packed with hydrangeas and reborn in a dining-room table display, they are full of life's joys.

OPPOSITE, INSET A Grecian urn-shaped vase is given a contemporary spin with a bouquet of sunny yellow roses.

Let yourself be seduced by booth after booth of shapely bowls, vases, and candelabra, handsome earthenware pots, dainty glasses, and pretty plates.

at markets and seem to be usurping their modern counterparts in many homes. This may be because vintage items introduce a bit of soul into clean-lined modern interiors—or because they retain an artistry that is lost in mass-produced pieces.

With decades of different styles to choose from, you will find pieces to satisfy your own taste. Go retro with chunky, funky 1950s pots, or go classical with large Roman pots. People with a penchant for global style can mix traditional English pale blue-and-white Wedgwood plates (which can also be valuable) with aqua-blue glazed tagines from the

Middle East. Country-style lovers will revel in the assortment of floral vases or striped ceramics. If minimalism is your thing, rummage for Japanese-style tea sets and celadon rice bowls to adorn otherwise naked windowsills.

While many ceramic and glass vessels have their conventional uses, you can create unusual features with everyday items. Chinese vases, for example, double as beautiful storage pots, while long-necked vases work as candelabra, and milk pitchers make elegant desk catch-alls. Old glass jars serve as beautiful lanterns for candles, as do other vessels,

OPPOSITE Display your glass jewels in a place where they can be properly admired. This collection of seconds and samples from a glassware factory adorn simple glass shelves. They have been placed in such a way as to catch the sun, so that a rainbow of light falls around a Plain Jane room.

particularly multicolored glass dessert bowls or blue-glass wine goblets. Extra large pieces, such as old Chinese vases or Arabic earthenware pots, can be transformed into umbrella stands.

Many ceramic or glass finds make original flower vases. Secondhand finds let you create startling, eye-catching looks with unusual pairings. Put big blooms in dainty teacups, for example, or gather a few gerbera in an old wine decanter. You could adorn eggcups with individual carnation heads or put pink roses in Moroccan tea glasses.

Old milk jugs, kitchen jars, tea caddies, large mugs, and teapots make unusual containers in which to grow parsley, sage, dill, basil, and other culinary herbs on a sunny windowsill. Grow a fern in a ceramic chamber pot, or crown a low-level vase with long grasses. For plants that need constant water, drill holes in the bottom of containers using a drill bit appropriate for the material. Put these planters on old saucers or big plain dinner plates.

Ceramic tiles are junk must-haves. When new owners move into a house, they frequently strip out old pieces in the cause of modernization, and beautiful orphans can be found at secondhand stores. These handmade pieces possess a warmth and workmanship that distinguishes them from their mass-produced counterparts. Look out for old white and blue Delftware tiles, graphic 1970s-style tiles, and traditional terracotta tiles. Being heat-resistant, these pieces can become useful coasters or hotplates. If you can find enough tiles of the same style (or mix your finds with new pieces), use them to make kitchen backsplashes or to add visual interest to bathroom tiles.

When buying your pieces, keep in mind where they will live. Remember that one beautiful piece is often more eye-catching than a cluster of items.

LEFT So kitsch—and yet so beautiful. A Japanese-style ceramic sculpture of a blossoming tree has been turned into a convenient jewelry stand, used to store—and to show off—the owner's collection of theatrical earrings.

Cherish your collections. A wall of plates, a window ledge of French milk pitchers, or a shelf of teapots can make a beautiful focal point.

ABOVE Invent new uses for old vessels. No longer needed as goblets, these gilt-edged Danish twins are now glamorous vases.

LEFT Cracked and chipped but by no means down and out, a pair of perfume bottles are born again as ornaments. To attract attention to their comely figures, they have been adorned with jewels and artificial butterflies.

ABOVE RIGHT Many glass tumblers, goblets, bowls, and dishes can be reused as candleholders, as exemplified by this petite, pretty glass beaker.

You will need to give your special piece enough space to breathe—place it in an alcove or against a white wall, for example; if it has star qualities, put it on show by shining a traditional brass picture light on it, or frame it with fairy lights.

If you want to group things on window ledges and shelves, buy pieces that vary in height and size and use the "family photo" principle, with large pieces at the back and small ones at the front. Mix rough with smooth, contrasting dark against light, and playing shiny pieces off matt pieces. Groups of items often grow organically. Once you have acquired a taste for an era, style, or type of object, you may find yourself inadvertently creating a collection of vases, teacups, eggcups, or glasses.

THIS PAGE From the ceramic serving plates to the silver coffee pot, this beautiful collection of kitchenware should prompt you to hurry down to your local market and scour the booths for classic items.

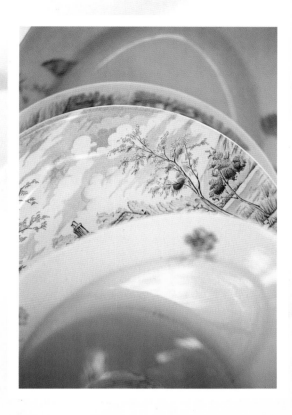

Items such as oversized copper pots, dainty crystal cake stands, tiny gold salt bowls with fine spoons, and solid–silver flatware were once so cherished that pieces were passed down through the generations—and now they are turning up at markets.

kitchenware

BELOW You can store rice, flour, sugar, cookies, pasta, and other groceries in vintage containers such as this assortment of kitsch, colorful retro tins.

Once upon a time, in an era before TV dinners, cooking, serving, and savoring food was a serious affair. The average time spent preparing evening meals was about one hour, while today it is less than a quarter of that time. Yet the rise of the TV dinner has proved a blessing for flea-market aficionados (and food lovers), who can now furnish their kitchens with beautiful, built-to-last cookware.

Many kitchen items have survived because they are robust, fashioned by artisans from good-quality materials. And there is something special about the warmth of a hand-painted bone-china cup that leaves a mass-produced mug in the shade. The errant line of a hand-beaten silver spoon has a more human quality than the over-smooth look of a piece straight off the factory production line.

Secondhand tableware will provide endless topics for dinner-party conversation. The discovery of each piece is often a story in itself. What's more, your finds may inspire culinary experimentation. If you like dinner parties with a twist, dine with 1970s-style fondue sets and heart-shaped gelatin molds.

Continuing the secondhand theme, serve food on an array of mismatching dinner plates. If you can't find a matching dinner set, create your own from pieces chosen according to color or pattern (all blue-themed plates, for example). You will also find a wealth of flatware at markets. Again, pick pieces of a similar style, delving deep for once-sought-after bone-handled utensils, which are lovely to hold (but not dishwasher-friendly), and three-pronged silver Georgian forks.

Serve your guests drinks from your found array of old tumblers, beer glasses and—for serious ale drinkers—Toby jugs. Scour markets for wine glasses with a similar look or shape, such as thin-stemmed red wine glasses with large bowls.

Champagne bowls reminiscent of *Breakfast at Tiffany's* sometimes put their pretty heads above the parapet at markets. These graceful glasses went out of fashion because the flute shape was found to keep champagne's bubbles for longer—but, if you believe that there is no reason not to quaff champagne quickly, invest in a set of mismatching bowls. Hunt down other drinks accessories such

OPPOSITE Once you start collecting orphaned pieces, you could soon find yourself with cupboards bursting with finds. This owner has collected items according to their culinary use—for example, oriental-style rice bowls and 1950s pastel-colored tea cups. Other collections include espresso cups, casserole dishes, salad bowls, milk pitchers, and dining plates.

as sherry decanters, ice buckets, ice tongs, wine coolers, waiter's corkscrews, and bottle openers.

One reason why antique glasses and ceramics have come back into fashion is the return of social occasions based on food rituals, such as coffee mornings and afternoon tea parties. Coffee lovers will find plenty of retro coffee pots and percolators as well as examples of wooden coffee grinders and branded coffee-bean jars. Graphically decorated cups and saucers are always good retro buys.

Secondhand markets also serve up an array of tea paraphernalia—themed teapots, tea cozies, milk jugs, delicate sugar bowls, sugar-cube tongs, and

ABOVE These eclectic finds have all been cherry-picked over years from the same big flea market in Brussels. The discerning owner has treasured pieces for their individual beauty, collecting shapes, colors and sizes from a range of different eras. Where possible, he has bought matching sets or hunted down groups of pieces with similar themes.

Antique glasses and ceramics have come back into vogue with the return of coffee mornings, tea parties, and other events based on food rituals.

OPPOSITE AND LEFT
Many divorced teacups turn up as singles at markets. Re-marry them to saucer finds, pairing gilt-edged floral cups with gilt-edged floral saucers, for example. Alternatively, use single teacups as tiny vases for single blooms or bouquets of wildflowers, or dot tea lights inside and use them as candle-holders.

RIGHT, ABOVE AND BELOW People who love baking will simply feast on market offerings. From old-style measuring spoons to themed-shaped cake tins and cookie cutters, there is a wealth of once-loved culinary items. Look for old wooden spoons, flour sifters, hand eggbeaters, and big ceramic bowls.

strainers—but what they do best is teacups. Your chance of finding a complete set is very slim, so look for pieces that harmonize, such as an assortment of gold-rimmed china cups or dainty floral designs. To serve accompanying cakes, snap up a 1950s crystal cake stand or a tiered stand in silver and pair it with an ornate silver cake knife.

When it comes to cookware, you will find plenty of examples of large wooden spoons, kettles, old copper pots, soup ladles, cookie cutters, ice-cream scoops, rolling pins, nutcrackers, old-fashioned egg beaters, and, with luck, old scales complete with measuring weights—as well as other kitchen paraphernalia (floral tin flour sifters with handles, measuring spoons, pressure cookers, glass juicers).

When you have acquired such beautiful old things, you definitely don't want to hide them in your drawers, so display lovely serving dishes on racks or hang your old-style copper pots and pans from a rack with butchers' hooks.

Lighting seems like a detail—yet nothing can transform a room as radically. Turn a spotlight on an elegant vase or light a single naked flame in a dark room—and notice how the whole room is born again.

lighting

OPPOSITE **Although this space is open plan, the two oriental-style, ball-shaped pendant lights define the dining space. The "masterpiece" behind the table is an old piece of patterned linoleum hung from bulldog clips on nails.**

RIGHT **Ornate glass-drop wall sconces, with a duet of golden pleated shades, create a glamorous focal point by day, and, with the engraved mirror behind, provide a warm wash of light by night.**

Let's start with the practicalities. When you are out shopping, there are three kinds of household lights to look out for: general lighting (for long dark nights), task lighting (for doing particular, close-up tasks), and feature lighting (for aesthetics).

The only caveat to bear in mind when buying secondhand light fixtures is to examine them for any signs of wear and tear such as exposed or loose wiring or bent socket pegs. If you have any doubts, get your lights checked and installed by a qualified electrician who can replace and rewire worn or damaged fixtures.

For general lighting, keep your eyes open for a range of lights, but take into account the shape, size, and function of the room in question. Living rooms are for relaxation and conversation, so the lighting in them needs to be soft and convivial, never brash, bright, or hospital-like. If your living room is pint-sized, create optical illusions with lights—for example, wall sconces provide a wash of light across the walls, making them appear larger. Eschew long-hanging or large bold pendant lights in small rooms because they tend to draw the eye downward, making ceilings seem lower.

General lighting should illuminate an entire room at the flick of a switch. It can take the form of wall sconces, floor lamps, or hanging fixtures, with or without shades. Wall sconces from all eras turn up at secondhand booths, since they are often orphaned when people tear out old fixtures to create clean lines in new homes. There is always a good selection of secondhand lamps at markets, some discarded from former factories or made redundant from offices. These pieces may require some tender loving customization, such as the repainting of a shade or the replacement of a base. If you discover a pendant shade that is the right size but not the right appearance, fashion your own cover from vintage fabric finds (think old curtains, secondhand skirts, or shawls), or customize it with ribbons, buttons, beads, or fake flowers.

One timeless secondhand find is a chandelier. Some come with cherubs and others have kitsch fake candles with flame-shaped bulbs, but the ones

ABOVE Avoid eye strain when reading in bed. Simply re-purpose an office desk light or a floor-standing lamp, which can be easily adjusted to direct light onto the book at hand.

RIGHT For an innovative reading lamp, use a clamp-on desk light on a chair's backrest, as shown here.

OPPOSITE An industrial-style floor-standing lamp suits the restrained style of this work space. While the owner could have repainted the light, its chipped and careworn looks complement the distressed paintwork of the rickety chair.

LEFT Elegant glass drops dangling from metal fronds have been added to an industrial light to form a "chandelier." Alternative, similar drops might include colorful beads, ribbons, or flower garlands.

BELOW This metal floral bouquet, of a type that came and went in a flicker during the 1950s, is a style of fixture that might see on your expeditions.

RIGHT If your horizons are global, seek out light shades such as this one, from a Moroccan market.

to look out for are original classics fashioned from shimmering, glamorous crystal. Snap up one of these to make any room feel a little decadent.

When it comes to task lighting, simply search for the right light for the job. For home offices, look out for gooseneck lamps, but make sure the springs are operational. If they are too loose, you will end up with a floppy light; if they are too tight, you won't be able to adjust them. In living rooms, you will need reading sidelights (or angled wall sconces) and in bedrooms, bedside reading lights. Think laterally. An old desk lamp could easily make a bedside table light. Table lamps are easy to create yourself. Introduce single items to each other to make beautiful marriages, such as an antique iron base and a funky 1950s shade, or a solid wooden base and a pleated pastel shade.

Feature lighting highlights a little of what you fancy. Use it to accent your most-loved possessions (use a downlighter, for example, to draw attention to a loved painting). Alternatively, you can choose old lights as pieces to adore for their own beauty. If you love a chandelier's sense of grandeur but don't want to wire it up, simply hang it near a window so it reflects the daylight. Other antique lights simply look handsome, such as ornate gas

THIS PICTURE **Just as diamonds are a girl's best friend, so chandeliers are a room's best friend. If it is too complicated to adapt your chandelier find to light a modern room, use it as decoration and hang it where the natural light can catch its sparkly drops.**

lights from yesteryear. For an air of otherworldly romance, look for strings of fairy lights. Some may require new bulbs or have missing decorations, so customize them with other finds, such as fake flowers or butterflies. If you want to accent pieces of artwork, search out traditional brass picture lights or frame a painting with fairy lights.

Most of your creativity will go into lighting your principal rooms, but keep the junk feeling alive in hallways and entrances and on staircases. It is easy to disregard these spaces, but funky lights help to make the most of what might otherwise be forgotten passageways. Dot mismatching second-hand lamps up the staircase, for example, or run a length of fairy lights down a hallway to create eye-catching features. Of course, first impressions

RIGHT Pair lighting finds like this lovely blue base with a vintage lampshade. If a base is in good shape but the shade is past help, re-cover the shade's frame with a vintage fabric or wallpaper find.

OPPOSITE Fairy lights can create alluring shapes on walls. If a set of fairy lights have lost their decorations, you could fashion your own light garland from artificial butterflies or flowers.

Create a magical, mystical atmosphere at night by dotting lit candles around the house—in clusters in corners of the bathroom, in lines across the mantelpiece—and lighting a solitary flame in the bedroom.

LEFT A cherub balances on her hand a quartet of long, thin candles, adding old-world glamour to a clean-lined modern kitchen.

count, so make sure your entranceway is well lit. This is the place to position one spectacular find, such as a customized chandelier or a big bold floor lamp with a graphic lampshade.

In conclusion, remember that the style of light that never dates is candlelight. There is nothing more evocative than a naked flame. While you may not find many wax candles at secondhand markets, you will find a glittering array of beautiful things to put them in—including old hurricane lanterns, oil lamplighters, and grand silver heirloom candelabra. Many unconventional discoveries, such as vintage bottles, old vases, colored tumblers, and crystal dessert bowls, also make beautiful candleholders.

OPPOSITE Collections can be whatever you want them to be. This mixture of fossils, flowerets of coral, silver cups, candleholders, trinkets and stuffed animals is the height of eclecticism.

RIGHT Tickle your fancy with fistfuls of colored feathers in glass jars.

If there are certain items that you are passionate about, you may find yourself buying one more . . . and another. Gradually the hunt reaches fever–pitch, and before you know it, you have acquired a collection.

collections and display

ABOVE Exhibit your loved things for all to see (but not for little fingers to touch) in glass-fronted cabinets.

RIGHT A beautiful effigy of the Virgin Mary models a selection of necklaces, while a group of pictures and portraits behind the statue preserves memories.

Creating a collection is about bringing together beautiful things that you adore and indulging your whims. Whether you are in love with oil paintings, peacock feathers, army buttons, vintage clothes, 1930s vases, antique jewelry, fake flowers, pop memorabilia, tin soldiers, or leather-bound poetry books, your hunt will take on a life of its own. Collecting brings out the hoarder in all of us.

Art collectors, for example, love markets, where whole galleries of pictures await them. Choose pieces by genre—old oil paintings, for example—or by theme, such as landscapes, flower displays, portraits, or dogs. Instead of just hanging pieces in conventional places, you could display them by grouping them on a wall or placing them on the floor along the length of a corridor. If you assemble a collection of pictures whose frames don't look right together, simply remove the frames and hang works from bulldog clips nailed to the wall or from clothespins clipped to an old washing line.

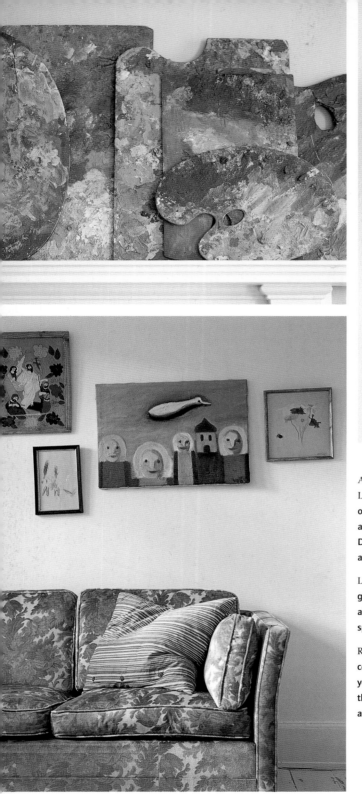

ABOVE AND ABOVE LEFT Markets are full of old oil paintings, but artists' palettes are rarer. Display your artistic gems against a canvas of white.

LEFT Hang pictures in groups for impact, but allow a bit of breathing space between them.

RIGHT Instead of using conventional frames, hang your photographs from the wall by bulldog clips attached to nails.

LEFT When you follow your instincts and make impulse buys at different markets, you will often end up, over time, with various examples on the same theme, such as this pack of dog portraits.

Otherwise, you could repaint the frames or replace them with beautiful alternatives, such as driftwood frames. For those who prefer photographic images, possible finds range from sepia-colored portraits to black and white landscapes. If your own ancestor collection does not amount to much, adopt other people's photographs by buying old family albums from markets. Unusual postcards can also be worth treasuring. To display memorabilia of this kind, string them up with paperclips or safety pins, or tack them onto walls to make a collage.

If you can't find any pieces of art or sculptures you like, devise your own masterpiece. Take, for example, one empty gilt frame and hang it on a blank wall. Within its gilt-edged boundary, simply tack up pieces you love, such as pinned butterflies or fake corsages sprayed with glitter dust—or create still-lives from personal mementoes such as coins acquired on foreign travels, dried roses, perfume bottles, or once-loved toys.

Mirrors, like paintings, look glamorous when grouped together, creating a feeling of light and space. Even a series of hand mirrors hung from a wall look stunning. Choose pieces with different

ABOVE Other finds for walls might include old maps, like the one shown here, pieces of vintage wallpaper, antique fabrics stretched over canvases, and linoleum offcuts.

shapes or similar frames, and use them to bring light into a dark corner like a stairwell or hallway.

Many fashionistas dedicate their flea-market legwork to finding beautiful vintage clothes as well as handbags, hats, shoes, and boots. Instead of letting these pieces languish like wallflowers in closets, put them on display. For example, you could clothe a dressmaker's form in your favorite

Many natural items turn up at markets—pieces of driftwood, coral, starfish, fossils, or semiprecious stones such as amethysts.

dress or simply hang much-loved pieces from coat hangers in open armoires or against closet doors. Display shoes from a series of miniature shelves or frame them in alcoves as if in a store. Hats and purses look dramatic when hung in groups from nails on the wall.

Other fashion accessories, such as feathers, fake corsages, brooches, lengths of ribbon, hairclips, lace, and dress pins, can be used to transform cushions, rugs, and other home accessories. If you discover some old brooches, for example, simply pin them onto one of your vintage pillows. Customize an old lampshade by tying a beautiful ribbon around it, or stick a series of feathers in its cap to give it instant panache. For a festive mood, create show-stopping garlands with a collection of

OPPOSITE, FAR LEFT AND CENTER Use found objects to fashion your own still life on a sideboard. Here, some old coffee tins have been given a decorative makeover.

OPPOSITE, RIGHT Display your vintage clothing collection on a dressmaker's form and change her dress weekly.

THIS PAGE Think about how to organize and show off your finds to best visual advantage. For example, pieces of found wood could be arranged in groups like long, thin ethnic figurines, as shown here, or made to stand to attention along a shelf (see inset).

LEFT AND RIGHT Instead of hiding your beautiful clothes, bags, and shoes behind closet doors, put them where they can strut their stuff. Display them along a wall on coat hangers hung from nails or picture hooks—or hang them from a metal kitchen rack. Recycle classic jackets and coats and keep your eyes peeled for good-quality, sturdy, wooden coat hangers.

BELOW Use capacious market bags as storage for your socks, lingerie, and handkerchiefs.

RIGHT Store beautiful little things—feathers, buttons, ribbons, thread, theatrical jewelry, string, buttons, safety pins—in glass jars and use them to customize your outfits or your home's interior. In this room, water pipes support an impromptu display of fake flowers, letters, and toys. From the pipes hang butchers' hooks festooned with Christmas baubles and necklaces.

artificial corsages strung together on a piece of colored string or a long length of ribbon. You could also hang and clip ribbons, artificial flowers and butterflies, and bead necklaces to wire coat hangers (weave a couple together by the handles) to create a mobile for a children's bedroom. If you have found a chandelier that has lost some of its drops, such *objets trouvés* make gorgeous replacements for the missing pieces.

Jewelry collections should never languish in a trinket box. Add glamour to walls, paintings, chairs, and headboards with strings of pearls, diamonds, opal pendants, and shimmering silver chains. If you have some glittery glass beads, string them up on windows and mirrors or over lampshades so that they reflect the light, sending little colored rays around the room.

Many natural items turn up at markets—pieces of driftwood, coral, starfish, fossils, or semiprecious stones such as amethysts. Put such natural wonders

LEFT AND BELOW
A collection of rosaries and crosses, some hanging from an ornate carved headboard, adds an air of spirituality to a bedroom.

FAR LEFT From old postcards and photographs to mirrors and necklaces, the collection of intimate images on this wall makes an original display.

where they can be appreciated or use them to create original works of art. Fashion driftwood into a photograph or mirror frame or drill tiny holes in a smooth, organic-shaped piece to put your sticks of incense in.

Most market aficionados are inevitably drawn toward the secondhand book and magazine section since there will always be something there to covet. From dusty copies of Charles Dickens's *Oliver Twist* to ancient Mickey Mouse comics, you are likely to discover something to stimulate your imagination on virtually every subject.

If you collect old magazines, you can always tear out pages and use them to make picture collages

RIGHT AND OPPOSITE Walls make wonderful canvases for the display of market-found objects such as beads, shell necklaces, old postcards, and hand-stitched lace. Other finds, such as dried flowers and autumn leaves, come from nature itself. Beautiful, fragile pieces like these allow you to create a "found" artwork against a plain backdrop.

to adorn your walls. Or, to enliven children's rooms, you could paste up pages from old comics to create original wallpaper that will absorb the little ones for hours. When it comes to displaying your literary finds, the conventional choices are bookshelves and office shelving, but for an alternative display you could stack your books, spines outward, in color-coded towers up and down a hallway.

Try to maintain the spirit of a collection in the way you display it. If you have gathered together fragile pieces—such as old perfume bottles, china figurines, or dainty teacups, for example—keep them protected from inquisitive small fingers by storing them in Art Deco cabinets with lockable glass doors. If you have decided to hoard early editions of classic books, think about storing them in a complementary weathered-wood bookshelf from a similar period—or contrast their fine old looks by showing them off in a plastic modern modular shelving system.

Instead of hiding your beautiful serving dishes at the back of your kitchen cabinets, display them as they would have been in former times on wooden racks, hung from the wall, or on country-style sideboards with display shelves. Look for a Victorian tea trolley on which to show off your dainty teacups, saucers, and teapots.

While many collections call for conventional display, think about how to arrange your treasured pieces in unusual places for maximum impact. Our eyes—like our ears—often fail to appreciate items that are presented to us in clichéd ways, so think about offbeat alternatives. If you have fallen for 1950s vases, for example, line the whole lot up like soldiers along the center of a table and crown them with big blooms. Or present your collection of old bottles by ranging them along a window ledge

(the light will highlight the glass), and fill your unused fireplace with vintage vases. Eye-catching pieces demand eye-catching displays.

If you collect odd bits and pieces, you will need to store them—and you could create a subsidiary collection from the boxes you put them in. You might, for example, buy a series of small leather suitcases in which to store a collection of costume jewelry or old coins—or you could use a roll of vintage wallpaper to cover cardboard boxes of all shapes and sizes. Old gym lockers, which provide generous storage, sometimes surface at markets, while mail-sorting shelves or stacked wine boxes could be transformed into open pigeonholes that will allow you to savor your much-loved finds.

putting it all together

Flea–market style is by its nature relaxing and comforting to live with because junk pieces with past lives are never precious, uptight, or pretentious; they have been there, done that—and lived to tell the tale.

relaxing spaces

LEFT Plenty of fabrics, from the floral cushion covers to the large skin on the floor, soften the feel of this industrial-style London warehouse. From the Guy Rogers daybed to the nut-brown Chesterfield sofa, all these pieces have been chosen for their classic looks. Ethnic finds, such as the Moroccan pouffe and the little African table add a note of eclectic chic.

When trying to create a relaxing space in flea-market style, the big backdrops— floors and walls—really count. If you want to include patterned furniture, make your backdrops plain; paint or paper walls in a neutral color and keep floors monochrome. If your living area is small, use optical illusion: light walls and floors will make the space look bigger, while dark canvases make the space look smaller. Mirrors double the light in a room, so harness their powers. Choose one large mirror (such as a former dressing-table mirror or full-length dressmaker's mirror) or create a mixture of styles by hanging a variety of mirrors on one wall.

If you like pattern but don't want to sacrifice a sense of space, decorate a single wall in vintage wallpaper, putting plain furniture in front of it. Strips of wallpaper or textured wallpapers also create funky backdrops. Consider stripped, stained, or painted wooden floors. Soften the look, and reduce noise, with textile finds such as old animal skins, including cowhides, goatskins, and sheepskins, and rugs, such as Indian dhurries, Persian prayer mats, and woven hearth rugs. Old carpets, which are frequently the first thing new owners strip out, also create foot-friendly floor covers. Simply cut them to the size you

Signs of having been loved—a coffee-cup blemish on a table, a worn patch on an armrest, a slight indent on a sofa—make flea-market finds easy to accommodate.

require. Your living room is one of the main public areas in the home, so it is worth taking time to style it to your satisfaction.

Most living rooms are organized around a single focal point such as a hearth, the home's traditional heartland. Seating is often grouped around a low-level table (think kidney tables, tables made from old railroad ties, retro chrome and glass tables). Arrange your furniture in groups for conviviality,

ABOVE **If you are lucky, you may stumble across design classics such as this red Ercol sofa, adorned with a jewellike collection of scatter cushions. An ethnic rug provides warmth and softness underfoot.**

with sofas facing each other or armchairs set in a circle. If you don't like sitting shoulder to shoulder with others on a sofa, then assemble a collection of slouchy armchairs; it won't matter that they don't match since they'll all share a laid-back look.

If your fireplace is meant to be a focal point, give it eye-catching style. Markets are home to old accessories, including wrought-iron fireguards, coal scuttles, copper bellows, cinder brushes, and pokers. The advent of the modern "hole-in-the-wall" fireplace has been responsible for many new homeowners stripping out beautiful old fireplaces and mantelpieces. Restore the glamour of an old fireplace, but before lighting up have the chimney inspected and cleaned by a professional, and bone up on the fuel-burning regulations in your area. Many urban areas require secondary burners for coal or wood fires to keep down pollution levels.

Lighting is the next priority. Living rooms need a combination of lights for different purposes. Apart from the vast choice of pendant lights on offer at markets, softer options include former office-desk lights for sofa-side reading and Victorian wall sconces for shining a wash of light on a wall, which has the bonus of making the room feel lighter and bigger. Everyone glows under the gentle light of a naked flame, so seek out discarded hurricane lamps or candleholders of all sorts.

The most important buys for your relaxing room are the pieces of furniture. Finding a sofa that fits you and your style has the same effect as buying a comfortable bed. When you get home, you'll never want to move. It is worth emphasizing that you should always try out furniture before making a purchase. A sofa, for example, may be good to look at, but if you sit on it, you may find that its springs are shot or its frame is broken. If you like lying on

THIS PAGE Juxtapose pieces with a similar feel. In this living room, timeless classics, from the black leather Chesterfield sofa (whose ripped arm is covered by a throw) to the ornate side table, combine to create a refined, elegant look. In the absence of a sideboard, the drinks have been stashed in a large wooden armoire.

THIS PAGE This sleek contemporary room is given a lived-in feel with found furniture. A chest of drawers, repainted white, provides storage, while a former desk offers a display surface for 1970s-style graphic vases.

THIS PAGE This living room, with its to-die-for beige leather sofa, looks eclectic but elegant. Its canvases—the white walls and glossy black floor—make the perfect backdrop for a sculptural lamp, a pillow fashioned from a silk scarf, and a portrait of Britain's young Queen Elizabeth II.

OPPOSITE **Create a haven for relaxation in an unexpected corner. In this guest bedroom, a chair upholstered in a soft, worn velvet cover makes an ideal place for repose. Peg rails, normally used in hallways, give extra hanging space for visitors' coats and bags.**

sofas, make sure that whichever one you plan to purchase is the right size. And, don't judge a sofa by its cover. You can always use vintage fabric finds or dyed sheets, ex-army rugs, and old curtains to re-upholster or re-cover an aged sofa. The repair process is not quite as simple in the case of leather sofas, since getting a leather sofa re-upholstered can be as expensive as buying a new one. If black leather is ripped or worn, you could patch it up with tape; if the arm of your brown leather sofa has started to look worn, wrap it in a cover. Many

of us have already adopted and developed styles for our interior spaces based on trends of the moment. One popular contemporary look combines old world glamour with a minimalist twist, for example. Paint your floorboards and walls white, then choose a couple of beautiful pieces, such as a large nut-brown leather sofa, an elaborate mirror or one eye-catching pendant light, and soften the look with cushions made from luxurious second-hand fabric discoveries, including pashmina shawls, cashmere jerseys, or silk dressing gowns.

ABOVE **Set against a backdrop of neutral floor and walls, this chintzy old sofa looks as good today as it did over 30 years ago.**

BELOW A self-confessed lover of flea-markets, the owner of this apartment has based his seating arrangement on two good-quality sofas fashioned out of stiff, resilient muslin. To protect their handsome visage, the sofas have been covered in thick blankets.

RIGHT Old leather club chairs sit comfortably side by side, flanking a classic lamp, originally designed for industrial use in the 1950s. Pieces like these are worth paying a little more for, particularly if they are in good condition, since they will retain their value.

Use vintage fabric finds, old curtains, or ex-army rugs to revive an old sofa.

Retro lovers will need to flip a few coins to choose between the wonderful range of sofas on offer. Low-level vinyl sofas or colored leather sofas were once all the rage. When teamed with 1960s wooden sideboards or plastic modular storage, these pieces swing again in their original living-room setting. Complete the look with cushions in graphic prints and vintage 1960s rugs or cuts of 1960s and 1970s carpets. Bean bags in good condition are also inviting.

When it comes to retro lighting, you can often find lights that fit the appropriate color scheme, such as, for example, plastic orange-shaded mushroom lights and large swooping floor chrome

THIS PAGE **This down-to-earth apartment in New York provides a perfect escape from the fast-pace of city life. One of its outstanding features is a pair of birdcages—a rarely spotted market find.**

lights (such as Castiglioni's "Swan" lamp). Markets are often full of chunky 1950s and graphic 1960s vases in which to show off flowers. Hang potted plants from the ceiling in macramé plant holders.

Devotees of Modernist and Bauhaus pieces will also, if they are fortunate, uncover 20th-century classics with which to enliven their relaxing spaces. Finds of this kind can sometimes be valuable.

ABOVE This classic buttonback sofa has been re-upholstered in thick, hard-wearing, former army blankets and accessorized with a Welsh blanket, a found cushion, and a jute-covered pillow. Hanging on the wall behind the sofa is a quirky collection of plates and pictures that have gone to the dogs.

THIS PAGE This sofa has received a makeover in the form of a canvas cover. For a deconstructed look, seams are left on the outside. To create a clash of eras, an elaborate old frame borders a modern painting. Two empty picture frames have been given a career change, becoming lightshades.

Originals or close reproductions of classics such as an Eileen Gray "Bibendum" chair, Arne Jacobson's "Swan" chair, Verner Panton's plastic "S" chair or Tom Dixon's "Jack" light turn up from time to time in markets. If you come across pieces of this kind in good condition, snap them up instantly because their value will only increase with time, while their looks remain timeless. More common pieces found at markets include bent chrome and leather chairs. Soften modernist lines with cow hides on the floor or sew cushions out of zebra prints.

Soften a minimalist look with cushions covered in luxurious secondhand fabric finds, including silk dressing gowns, pashmina shawls, or cashmere jerseys.

LEFT A soft, dreamy light filtering in through lace curtains gives this relaxing space an ethereal feel. Covering the generously large sofa is an old linen sheet, while a shawl is draped casually over its arm.

ABOVE RIGHT A gorgeous modern rug has been fashioned out of a patchwork of cow hides. Propped up against the wall is a bestselling print of *The Chinese Girl* by the Russian artist Vladimir Tretchikoff.

If you hanker after a country look, flea-market finds will fulfil your rustic desires. Since your most expensive purchase for a relaxing space is likely to be a sofa, choose one that optimizes the look—such as a large, slightly saggy version covered with loose linen chintz—and pile it with crocheted or plaid blankets. If your discovery is the correct shape but simply needs a new dress, clothe it in striped ticking fabrics or a hardwearing canvas. Chairs to complete the look include old rocking chairs, wicker Lloyd Loom chairs, patio-style wooden chairs, and benches made out of rustic woods.

If you require side tables for vases, books and table lights, look for school desks and outdoor furniture such as wrought-iron garden tables with mosaic tops. Posies of wildflowers and bouquets of roses in odd found vessels such as bone-china tea cups, rustic French milk pitchers, and vintage bottles bring life and freshness to your space.

Relaxing spaces are not limited to living rooms. Other places of relaxation at home include nooks and crannies such as the end of a hallway, a space under the stairs, or a large stair landing. Wherever it is quiet or where the sunlight falls is potentially a place to park. Flea markets offer equally odd pieces on which you can recline, including colorful canvas hammocks, homemade swings, roll-out tatami mats, and even blow-up mattresses. Since you are a flea-market shopper, you must be used to thinking outside the conventions of a matching three-piece suite, so seek out something original, something that will really help you to relax.

Flea-market style will give a kitchen a cherished and lived-in feel. From big old cookie tins to solid coffee pots and huge frying pans, formerly loved pieces add to the kitchen's magnetism.

cooking & eating spaces

LEFT AND ABOVE RIGHT There is no need for kitchen pieces bought at flea markets to match. Secondhand finds will allow you to create an original space with timeless furnishings and accessories for next to nothing.

You could, if you wanted to, furnish your cooking and eating spaces with almost everything sourced from flea markets—including the kitchen sink. One good reason for doing so is the sense of tradition that market-found objects bring to these spaces. Most of us continue to cook and eat as we always have, but time spent preparing meals has steadily diminished. While the generation of home cooks before us spent up to an hour each night preparing the family meal, our increasingly fast-paced lives have reduced this time to mere minutes.

But, however long food takes to cook or prepare, the majority of us still love the rituals of dining—relishing, for example, the solid feel of thick silverware, the taste of water poured into tumblers from an elegant glass pitcher, and the bouquet of wine served from thin-stemmed, wide-bowled wine glasses. And we are still magnetized by the feel-good warmth of a big kitchen table.

Where cooking and eating rooms were customarily separate, in modern homes they are often rolled into one big space, in which the eating area combines with

ABOVE Mismatched chairs, retouched in pastel shades of eggshell paint, sit attentively at a long, thin table covered by a found yellow linen table runner. Dried hydrangea heads in former graveyard vases add to the faded, otherworldly beauty of this sun-filled eating space.

the food preparation area, farmhouse-style. And, while a kitchen table is used for food preparation and the eating of meals, it is also the place where people gather for long conversations, homework, games, or other leisure activities.

When it comes to furnishing your cooking and dining space, the first thing you need to do is decide what kind of look you want to achieve. If you already have a sleek contemporary kitchen, you can add a handful of vintage one-offs to give it a little soul. Contemporary custom-made kitchens can

look high-tech and clinical, but old pieces give them depth and character. And these slick, modern kitchens make clean-lined canvases against which you can show off your fabulous finds.

Modern doesn't have to mean buying new. For a modern classic look in the kitchen, keep the feel minimalist, hiding clutter behind smooth cabinet doors. Display finds such as one curvaceous 1960s vase with flowers on a mantelpiece, and if you do show your kitchenwares, make sure they are classic (a silver kettle or a Romanesque water pitcher, for

THIS PAGE **The centerpiece of this eating area is a 1950s conference table created for office use. Polished and adorned with a pair of old candelabra, it is now a stylish dining table.**

RIGHT **Many cooking, eating, and relaxing spaces are now rolled into one large flowing area. In this home a 1970s sofa bed mixes with an antique high chair, wooden café chairs, and old copper pans.**

example), elegant (secondhand champagne flutes or a tall retro coffee pot), or space-enhancing (a shiny silver milk pitcher or a chrome toaster).

Add depth to a contemporary eating space by adorning your swanky, purchased, glass-top table with one beautiful antique candelabrum. There's no need to buy new chairs when secondhand markets are overflowing with an array of modern classics such as bent chrome and leather chairs, bentwood café chairs, and molded-plastic 1960s chairs. You can always fashion your own dinner table from a smooth, repainted door mounted on trestles or an old boardroom table.

If you want to clad a modern table in a classic gown, look out for white linen and damask napery (matching tablecloth and napkins). Once given as wedding presents or passed down as heirlooms, these beautiful sets make rare appearances at markets. If you can't find a set, an ensemble of non-matching napery is easy to create and looks just as good. Crown your table with a glamorous centerpiece such as a stunning vase of flowers or a low-hanging, glittering chandelier.

RIGHT The table is a market find that has been given a chic zinc top. On the table, a small blue cast-iron pot makes a funky vase.

FAR RIGHT Revive cupboards by painting doors in a rainbow of colors and give them chi-chi handles, as seen here.

OPPOSITE The dining room in the same house combines contemporary classics with antique finds. On the swanky boardroom-style chair is a pillow fashioned from a vintage Christian Dior scarf. On the 1970s table is an antique Indian pot with a single white flower.

THIS PAGE The sleek, chic kitchen in a London house shows how to mix retro style with modern lines. Without the beautiful candelabra in the corner and the painting—which takes its inspiration from an old silk scarf—this contemporary kitchen would simply lack spirit.

If you already have a sleek contemporary kitchen, you can adorn it with a handful of vintage flea-market finds to give it a little soul.

A country-style kitchen is particularly well suited to flea-market finds—right down to the kitchen sink (a butler sink, of course). For the walls, look for tongue-and-groove paneling, terracotta tiles, or vintage floral wallpapers. For storage, choose freestanding pieces such as unpainted cupboards and old plate racks. Fabrics are an integral part of the country look, so scour markets for traditional country patterns (think floral, paisley, or gingham) and fashion these pieces into tablecloths, curtains, tea towels, or aprons. Create under-sink storage with a colorful curtain strung on a wire.

If you collect country-style kitchen accessories, make a display of them. Pieces of enamelware, collections of old copper pots, wooden chopping boards, handmade pottery, patterned plates, old coffee grinders, and big copper kettles need to be showcased from like-minded shelves and cupboards such as old bookshelves, armoires with no doors, and old laundry racks lashed to the ceiling.

Secondhand stoves and reconditioned ranges sometimes turn up at markets, but it pays to have such major fixtures overhauled and installed by a professional. An old shallow butler sink or deep ceramic sink accessorized with brass faucets is another way to take your kitchen to the country.

For country-style eating spaces, start with a big, big table. You may find a large farmhouse or refectory table—or look for extendable pinewood tables or former boardroom tables to cover with a vintage tablecloth. For country-style seating, choose folding garden chairs, distressed painted chairs, or an assortment of wooden chairs. Large benches, like big tables, bring people together, so look for old church pews or school benches to seat your dinner guests (soften hard seats with squab cushions covered in vintage fabrics).

ABOVE A plain backdrop allows for a subtle play of pattern and color. The 1970s table is covered with floral vintage bark cloth.

OPPOSITE A pair of found bar stools transform a counter into a breakfast bar. The antique silverware is a collection of found single pieces, while the Moroccan tea glasses are a typical market find.

If you long to create a retro look, you need to go no farther than your nearest market. You may be fortunate enough to unearth Formica-topped cupboards and sideboards from the 1950s as well as retro refrigerators. If not, many chain stores sell good reproductions, which you can easily accessorize with finds such as colorful melamine plates, cups, and bowls, graphically decorated or pastel-colored china, retro toasters and kettles, and kidney-shaped fruit bowls and vases. For a 1950s look, choose pieces in pastel. If it's a 1960s vibe that you are after, go for bold brassy colors (red, yellow, purple) and bold patterns.

Markets will also furnish your retro dining space. Scour booths for retro furniture pieces such as round plastic tables with matching molded chairs, curvy wooden chairs, and oval wooden tables. For total authenticity, serve drinks from a low-level wooden 1960s sideboard or wheel them in on a trolley. Clothe your table with tablecloths sewn from retro fabrics such as florals and candy stripes from the 1950s, graphic circles and swirls from the 1960s, or graphic fruit patterns from the 1970s.

Cooking and eating spaces are also happy to accommodate an eclectic look that consists of mismatched but beautiful objects. The common denominator will be your taste. While an all-out eclectic look can work (modern and classic, high tech with old tech), you may find that your own style falls into a new genre. Many markets are full of goods and food ideas from around the world, including chinoiserie tea caddies, tagine dishes, jade chopsticks, large Japanese soup bowls, Indian thali dishes, and old French stewing pots.

Use your eye—and your tastebuds—to create your own eclectic look. "Global ethnic," for example, might be reflected in a very simple and utilitarian cooking space with accessories such as Moroccan tea glasses, earthenware pots, and Ethiopian coffee

LEFT An old tin makes a beautiful container for a bouquet of amaryllis. This old farmhouse-style table and its accompanying quartet of ex-café chairs are all classic market finds.

ABOVE Once at home in a hunting lodge in France, this long thin table makes a convivial dining spot. The old school chairs, made comfortable with cushions covered in vintage floral fabrics, were cast-offs from a local coffee-shop.

RIGHT The crowning glory of this dining room is an exquisite chandelier, found in almost mint condition in a market. The antique mirror behind reflects its beauty, turning an ordinary space into something extraordinary.

pots, while the eating space is informal, focused on a low-level, Arabic-style table, with colorful cushions strewn all around. To create a low-level table, simply saw the legs off a taller one; to make your own pillow collection, sew antique Indian saris into cushion and bolster covers for your guests to sit on. Source goods from local ethnic markets as well as markets you come across on your travels.

Whatever your style, flea markets will give you the opportunity to indulge in long-neglected dining customs. Revive fads such as 1970s fondue parties, cake decorating, pressure-cooking, coffee mornings, or the rituals of old-fashioned afternoon tea. You can serve tea out of bone-china cups and cake from a cake stand, find old lace doilies for plates, and adorn your teapot with a knitted tea cozy.

THIS PAGE AND OPPOSITE This kitchen is full of otherworldly charm, its plain visage transformed with beautiful vintage things. Pieces of old wallpaper, antique postcards, and sepia-toned photographs are stuck with masking tape to a perfectly ordinary refrigerator. The ceramic sink, the bentwood chairs, and the metal dish rack add to its glamorous but careworn looks.

When it comes to shaping your cooking and eating areas, be honest about your needs. If you really do cook and eat on the run, then pick flea-market finds to suit your lifestyle as well as your style. If you live alone but like to host occasional dinner parties, choose flexible pieces, such as tables with drop leaves or slide-away leaves and folding chairs. If you live alone and eat out all the time, turn your back on a big cook–eat space and go for a breakfast-bar arrangement instead. Perch at a high counter on market-found bar stools or old laboratory stools. If TV dinners are your thing, look for breakfast trays, large coffee tables, and low-level sofas so you can sit down, relax, and feast on your take-out in secondhand style.

THIS PAGE **To sleep, perchance to dream, in a room full of finds. When the sleeper wakes from her slumber between old linen sheets, she steps out onto a piece of foam covered by vintage fabric. To soften the minimalist style of the bedroom, all the pieces of furniture are made from warm-to-touch woods.**

If you can't decide what style of bedroom you really want, keep an open mind and let the pieces you find at markets dictate the look.

sleeping spaces

Sleep the sleep of kings in your bedroom, and do it in secondhand style. While bedrooms are intimate spaces, they also say much about us as individuals —just walk into any bedroom and deduce from the style and state of the room what kind of person inhabits it. Markets can help you express yourself in your bedroom. And, in a bedroom styled to reflect just who you are, you can sleep easily.

Picture this. In your room is a headboard built out of an old gate, a rickety garden chair bought from a sunny Sunday estate sale, and a cushion fashioned from a headscarf cherry-picked from a Paris flea market. Each individual item says so much about who you are and what you love. That's what makes your boudoir exclusive.

When it comes to arranging and furnishing your bedroom, there are some tried-and-tested styles to choose from. To save time and money, keep in mind the overall style that you are attempting to achieve, since this will influence your purchasing decisions. If you can't decide on a style, maintain an open mind and let the pieces you find dictate the look.

If you strike it lucky, you may find, for example, a beautiful *lit bateau* or a four-poster bed under dusty covers. With such an object as the centerpiece of a room, you will naturally want to hunt down items to harmonize with its sassy style, such as a sparkly antique chandelier, heirloom linen sheets, a silk kimono, or an ornate chaise longue.

A minimalist style is popular in bedrooms because there is something quietly relaxing about those pared-back lines and lack of clutter. To keep the space simple, all you need is a few big and beautiful things. The rest

LEFT If you discover a beautiful bed frame but can't find a mattress to fit, you can do as this owner has done and fit a single divan within a queen-sized frame. The fabric on the bed and the dust ruffle are crafted from vintage fabrics, while the pillow is made from canvas sacking.

Special finds make most impact when they strike an unexpected pose. Hang a patchwork quilt on a wall, for example, or turn it into a makeshift curtain.

ABOVE Pale bedding and furnishings give this small bedroom a spacious, light, and airy feel. The curtain and the dust ruffle, from the same bolt of satin damask, add glamour.

LEFT Crisp white cotton pillowcases make a neutral contrast to this ethnic quilt. On the wall, family photos are mounted on bulldog clips attached to tiny pins. If you don't have enough photos of your own, you can buy albums from markets. A top hat is used as a desk caddy.

of the room can be left naked. Start by making neutral backdrops of the floors and walls (strict minimalists keep to white or off-white), but try to avoid creating too much starkness; you can soften the look with plenty of fabrics, using pattern and color to magnetize the eye. One colorful silk pillow on a bed, for example, a cow hide on the floor or a white handmade lace shawl over the window is all you need to bring in warmth.

Unless you are lucky enough to have a separate dressing room, your bedroom will probably double as a dressing room. For lovers of minimalism, this means that efficient storage is vital. To create streamlined space, you could conceal clothes and accessories in one enormous armoire, painted in simple colors or left in its natural state. Oversized

THIS PAGE Why buy a
big lumbering armoire
when you can hide your
clothes behind curtains
made from vintage fabrics?
In this bedroom, small
clothing items are stowed
beneath a bed in deep
wooden trays that have
been repainted in funky
colors and given handles.
The look here is East-meets-
West, where traditional
floral comforters have
been teamed with oriental
paper lampshades.

THIS PAGE The clever-storage story continues. On an old strip of paneling fashioned into a shelf sit capacious bags that were found at an Indian market. Decapitated Indian tins have been stuck onto the wall to provide peep-show bedside shelving for books and ornaments.

armoires—and often crafted from beautiful old hardwoods such as oak, mahogany, and cherry—turn up regularly at markets because many new owners banish them from their homes in favor of contemporary-style floor-to-ceiling storage. When choosing a bed, look for one stunning piece with a plain or ornate white headboard. Dress the bed in light, airy, white neutrals, such as pure linen sheets. While intact antique linens can be found at many markets, you could also fashion your own minimal-style comforters out of a patchwork of white linen sheets.

There is something unpretentious and down-to-earth about country style's soft, faded look that is completely at home in bedrooms. A bedroom's star is the bed, so choose from wrought-iron bedsteads, old hospital beds, and wooden beds to work this look. Keep bed-frame paintwork in honest white or leave it distressed.

When it comes to clothing your bed, there are plenty of rustic choices, from floral duvet covers to crocheted patchwork blankets and old eiderdowns with sateen covers. You can use eiderdowns as wall hangings or window covers if they are exceptional pieces. To revive an eiderdown, simply take it to the drycleaner or hang it on a clothesline in the sunlight for a day and follow up with a shake and a good vacuum.

Like big-floral dresses and gumboots, patchwork has always been part of country-style interiors. To create your own works, study old patchwork quilts to see how many are sewn out of scraps of clothes such as floral dresses, silk scarves, striped shirts, tweed suit jackets, and embroidered baby clothes. When creating your own masterpiece, scour vintage clothing markets for pieces like these, but also keep your eyes open for conventional fabric furnishing

ABOVE Use texture to soften pared-back lines in a minimalist room. This plain door, for example, has been given a feminine twist with its cover of flock wallpaper. Show off your vintage designer clothes against a stark white backdrop.

RIGHT Every bed should be well dressed. While the trousers hanging over the end of the bed may be this year's Gucci, the beautiful pillows are yesteryear's silk scarves. Necklaces strung from the headboard complete the outfit.

finds, such as striped cotton ticking, gingham tablecloths, and floral bedspreads. Instead of comforters, you can clothe your bed with lovely old woolen blankets, such as plaid throws and former army blankets. Country patterns—paisley, floral, stripes, and ginghams—can also be used to make curtains, cushions, and chair covers. If you want an abundance of pattern, remember to avoid visual overload by keeping the backdrop plain.

When it comes to storage, maintain the same themes by choosing distressed armoires, painted

bookshelves, and old wooden dressers. If you need alternative storage, use your country-style woven shopping bags, wicker hampers, tea chests, and old suitcases. If you have room, consider acquiring an antique rocking chair, a wicker garden chair, or a chocolate-brown leather armchair.

While bedrooms are designed for rest, they are also places for romance. Turn your room into a chic boudoir with pieces to please the senses. Create a come-hither space with tactile textures and seductive furnishings. While it is unusual to find a four-poster bed at a market, you could build your own out of old boards, draping saris or silk scarves from the posts. Headboards are crucial to this look. Create your own by stretching a found fake animal skin across a length of board or restore an old rococo-style headboard. Create an air of luxury with too many pillows in an assortment of sizes and shapes. To complete the scene, put a classic

THIS PAGE Two single-bed finds have been joined to create one large bed. Two distinctive treasures—the ornate 1980s side lamp and the antique bedside cabinet—add a luxurious look to this loft bedroom.

THIS PAGE Import off-beat pieces into sleeping spaces to enhance their character. Here, a garden bench serves as a bedside table and a gooseneck desk light serves as a bedside lamp. A vintage tablecloth makes a chic alternative bedcover.

THIS PAGE A metal floral lamp, a vintage scarf draped over a lamp, an angel cookie cutter, and an open fan are just a few of the disparate things that, strangely, feel just right together in this calm, lived-in space. Plenty of white strikes a deal for peace with the multipattern mix.

piece of furniture alongside the bed, such as an old chaise-longue or a Louis XVI-style armchair.

For a luxurious feel next to the skin, look for silk sheets at markets. For your bed cover, see if you can find velvet or velveteen curtains, popular in the 1980s, to fashion into oh-so-soft cushions or bedspreads. To complete this glamorous, sexy look, think lighting. Crown your room with one extravagantly large, low-hanging chandelier, or put gothic wall sconces above the bed instead of bedside lights. Pleasure seekers will make sure they

ABOVE Groovy bedroom, baby. This 1970s bed, with its headboard in the shape of car seats, is flanked by lengths of vintage floral fabrics to create the feel of an intimate four-poster in this airy warehouse. While you are running up the curtains, why not make a couple of skirts to rock around the house in, as this owner has done?

get out on the right side of the bed each day by letting their feet step onto a sensuously soft rug— an old shag-pile carpet cut into a rug or a dyed sheepskin rug, for example.

If your style is more offbeat, seek out retro finds. Much of this particular quest is about discovering the right accessories, such as graphically decorated fabrics for bed covers, headboards, upholstery, and cushions. Looks of the 1950s overlap a little with country style, which can be feminine at heart, especially if you go for the era's soft pastels—baby pinks, pea greens, and lemon yellows—combined with chintzy florals and paisleys. For a 1960s vibe, mix big graphic prints on accessories derived from the vintage clothes, curtains, and bedspreads. If pieces from the 1970s interest you, indulge your inner hippy and find a kaftan to use as a bathrobe, dress your bed in an Indian cotton bedspread, and put a colorful dhurry rug on the floor.

For retro storage, search for low-level closet sideboards. Instead of a conventional wardrobe, hide your clothes behind one large piece of vintage fabric strung up from a wire. If you are a collector of vintage clothes, why hide them at all? Display your prized pieces against a backdrop of white.

Alternatively, you can simply create your own look from flea-market discoveries by mixing and matching different styles and eras. Pieces used in unconventional ways—a side table crafted from a repainted stool, a fold-out garden chair covered by a lace scarf, an old school desk with the legs sawn off—make eye-catching statements. Use an old

sewing-machine trestle in place of a dressing table and find a Venetian-style mirror to lean against it.

Secondhand markets are also full of handy storage items, including good-quality coat-hangers, wooden suit-hangers, jewelry and trinket boxes, hatboxes, shoehorns, shoe racks, lavender sachets, and large wicker laundry baskets. You will find yourself lingering over stalls of beautiful, memory-evoking items from the past, such as old photographs, Chinese fans, pinned butterflies, oil paintings, and piles of vintage magazines. Any of these can be used to embellish your bedroom walls.

Once you have hunted down all the things that make you feel at home, curl up and go to sleep. After all, shopping is such hard work.

ABOVE LEFT A brightly colored patchwork blanket from a baby's crib adds a slash of visual interest to a minimalist bedroom. Strips of floral and striped fabrics have been sewn together to make the curtain.

ABOVE For a little luxury, track down an original kimono to swan around in, like the red one seen here. A pretty lace panel makes an eye-stopping, light-enhancing window cover.

THIS PAGE **If you uncover old bed ends like these, snap them up and fasten them to a modern bed. Cover any under-bed sins with a dust ruffle, which you can create from fabric bolts, tablecloths, or old bedspreads. To show off finds, create a gallery "space" such as these built-in shelves, exhibited to a rhapsody in blue.**

THIS PAGE Bathrooms should be relaxing places, devoted to the revival and refreshment of body and soul. From the gentle, off-white color scheme to the market-found accessories—a tin-saucer soap dish, a former living-room mirror, and an ethnic wooden stool—everything in this room is conducive to calm.

RIGHT Every bathroom needs a mirror, so, if you come across one whose shape you like but whose frame is dull, all you may need to do is to repaint it.

Bathrooms are intimate and sensual spaces—one of the few really private places in the home—so make them yours with things you love.

bathing spaces

Traditionally, bathrooms have been treated as an afterthought in the design and decoration of a home. Unlike kitchens and living rooms, they are private, intimate spaces, often tucked away in dark, pint-sized rooms. While bathrooms are primarily functional, we are now demanding that they should also be havens of peace, so that we can soothe away all our cares behind their closed doors.

That is where flea-market style comes in. The items that can be found at markets—large rolltop bathtubs, large Victorian showerheads, antique mirrors—all look beautiful, extolling a careworn, lived-in look. And, while it is important to get your bathroom's functional elements right, the pieces you will pick up at markets will help you to get the aesthetics right so that you can use your steamy sanctuary for genuine, deep relaxation.

Start with the room's backdrops, the floors and walls. Many bathrooms are located in the smallest, darkest rooms in the home. If this is true in your case, use optical illusion to make the space seem bigger. To "create" space, you need to maximize the light in the room, so make large surfaces glossy and the overall color scheme light and bright.

The need for lightness extends to floors, which can be covered with reclaimed tiles or lengths of pale antique wood. The shinier the floor, the more light it will reflect, so coat your floorboards with a

THIS PAGE With its pink, blue, and white color scheme, the overall look of this room is peaceful and reassuring. The candy-colored, woven-plastic chair is both attractive and waterproof. A former magazine rack provides bathside reading storage.

THIS PICTURE A glass-fronted cabinet repainted tranquil blue is filled with quirky, witty objects for the bather to admire. Its mirrored back reflects light around the room and enhances the feeling of space in the room.

ABOVE LEFT At the end of the day, nothing is more soothing on the eye than the soft, warm light of candles. These stand in old enamel lamplighters.

LEFT This crocheted blanket and vintage vest are common market finds, which provide handy post-bath wear. Laundry often ends up in bathrooms so store it in a container like the string bag seen here.

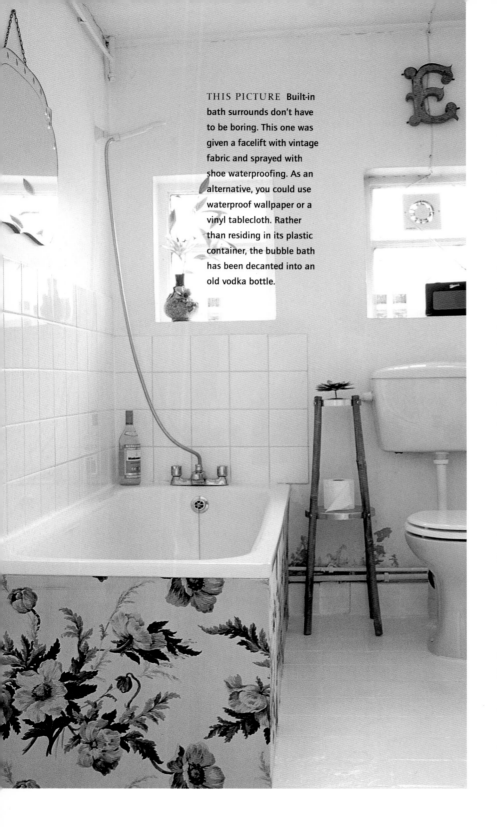

THIS PICTURE Built-in bath surrounds don't have to be boring. This one was given a facelift with vintage fabric and sprayed with shoe waterproofing. As an alternative, you could use waterproof wallpaper or a vinyl tablecloth. Rather than residing in its plastic container, the bubble bath has been decanted into an old vodka bottle.

glossy varnish. Linoleum, currently back in vogue, is one of those floorings many people strip out of their new homes in favor of more contemporary floor coverings, but the good news for finders is that lino is a hard-wearing, splash-proof, child-friendly flooring. If you can't find enough to cover your floor, simply cut off a strip to use as a mat in areas prone to splashes and spills.

When you step out of your luxurious bath, you will want to step onto a bathmat that is kind to the soles of your feet. It is possible to find mats made from original duckboard slats, old shag-pile toweling, or cork. Alternatively, make one from a thick towel or a piece of carpet—or use a rug.

White tiles are functional and beautiful on walls. Even if you opt for new tiles, keep your eyes open for off-beat secondhand tiles to break up the too-smooth look of new tiles. For example, you could create a patchwork of old white-and-blue Delft tiles (often stripped out of Victorian bathrooms) or add a strip of colorful Moroccan mosaic tiles. For a rustic feel, panel your walls in reclaimed wood.

A bathroom wall's ornaments are its mirrors. While you need mirrors for daily bathroom rituals, you can also, by strategic positioning, use them to harness the spatial powers of light. If you find a mirror that's the right shape but has an ugly frame, repaint the frame in a color to suit your room or make one yourself out of natural objects such as seashells, sand-colored pebbles, or driftwood. If you have limited wall space, you could give wall-mounted bathroom cabinets a shiny new mirrored face to help enhance the light.

The centerpiece of most bathrooms is, of course, the tub. One of the most popular fixtures, which brings with it an air of luxury and indulgence, is an antique cast-iron, claw-footed, rolltop bathtub. If

For a bathroom with a sense of humor, dress your toilet in a kitsch, colorful terrycloth seat cover and paint the outside of the tub and the vanity in contrasting colors.

If there is enough room, other pieces of furniture can be used to add to the feeling of repose, such as generously large armchairs, chaise longues, or daybeds. Apart from adding to the comfort and luxury of the room, such seating makes it easier to carry out beauty routines such as pedicures and facials. Small tables, such as former coffee tables

Give a new tub character with a siding of vintage wallpaper, reclaimed boards, or a patchwork of old tiles.

you find a tub with chipped or cracked enamel, you can get it re-enameled—but remember that this can double its original price. Look for reconditioned faucets and spout fixtures, which you should get installed by a professional plumber. If you find a tub with broken legs, simply remount it on slats of antique reclaimed wood or breeze blocks.

Even in a bathroom, flea-market style defies tradition. If you reject the idea of conventional matching appliances, your bathroom could be a happy mismatch of reclaimed bathtub, basin, and toilet. You could marry an old copper tub with a Victorian toilet and a washstand backed with old tiles, or combine a rolltop tub with a deep ceramic sink and a toilet with a reclaimed mahogany seat.

THIS PAGE A calm display to bathe by is dominated by an empty picture frame and a picture of a nude with downcast eyes, both sitting alongside dishes, blocky vases, and an heirloom candleholder on a wooden work bench.

OPPOSITE Among the beautiful finds in this room are the ceramic sink with antique faucets, the "tables" (crates balanced on their ends), and the necklace-draped mirror.

or wrought-iron garden tables, provide surfaces for stacks of towels, fresh flowers, or your collection of lotions and potions.

For total relaxation, the view from the bathtub needs to be uncluttered, so make it possible to keep everything cleared away by installing ample storage. You will find former bathroom cabinets at markets and you can import other storage ideas from around the home. Pile your towels into old armoires or chests of drawers, and house your toiletries and elixirs in old medicine cabinets or an unused bedside drawer unit.

When it comes to small storage, market finds have infinite uses. For example, you can use old pails or topless olive-oil cans as wastebaskets and put your toothbrushes in vintage vases or old colored-glass tumblers. Pile toilet paper in old shopping baskets or hatboxes and use sculptural ashtrays and delicate china saucers as soap dishes.

Old grooming items sometimes turn up at markets, including manicure sets, hand mirrors, eyelash curlers, bone-handled hairbrushes, curlers, and shaver brushes. These implements are often sturdy and built to last, and do the job much better than their flimsy contemporary counterparts.

With all your clutter swept away, the next thing is to evoke a calm, peaceful atmosphere. A small posy of flowers in an old china tea cup or a leafy green plant in an old chamber pot will give you something living and breathing to look at. You can also bring yourself back to earth with finds from nature, such as pieces of coral, conch shells, fossil swirls, and pieces of sculptural driftwood.

The flickering, warm light of a flame is soft on tired eyes so, for an ultra-soothing effect, transform your bathroom at night into a grotto of candles. Place your candles in old storm lanterns, elegant

oil lamps, or graceful antique candelabra, or dot tealights in Moroccan tea glasses around the room.

To enhance your privacy, use beautiful window coverings to exclude prying eyes while maintaining an aesthetically pleasing look. To let light diffuse through the curtains, source pieces such as lace shawls and linen tablecloths, or create a patchwork curtain from old silk scarves in pale colors.

ABOVE A shower alcove has been tiled with second-hand tiles and accessorized with vintage towels.

RIGHT A saunalike feel has been created in this bathroom by the use of reclaimed wood.

THIS PICTURE What was originally a hospital crib has been sprayed with colorful paints to give it a new lease on life. While it's easy to indulge your inner child, try to avoid color overdrive. Remember that bedrooms are where your children unwind and relax. Use plenty of white space to strike a balance.

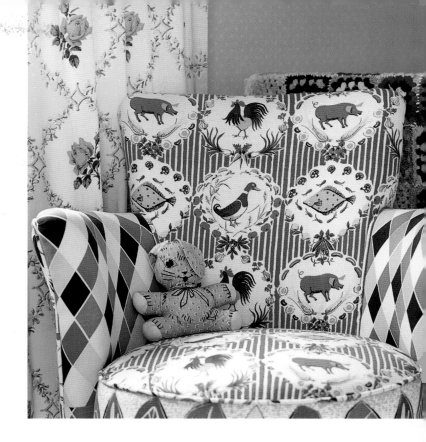

When it comes to decorating your child's bedroom, flea-market style says, "Come on, let's play." There's something about finding furniture for children's rooms that allows us to let our inner child have free rein.

children's spaces

Children's spaces are their studies and bedrooms—or, if you are lucky, a separate rumpus room. In most cases, children's play areas spill into parents' living areas, so, to keep the rising tide of primary-colored toys at bay, good storage is vital. To keep your adult living space looking sane, hunt for finds such tea chests, trunks, suitcases, wicker baskets, and laundry baskets that will fit in with your décor.

In your child's bedroom, however, you can let your hair down. It is a good idea to keep walls and floors neutral since children's tastes change like the wind. Let today's favorite pictures and posters of cartoons, animals, and rock stars blow in and out onto blank spaces. The overall feel should be

a relaxed one since the bedroom is where a child unwinds. Children love bright color schemes, but temper loud colors with plenty of deep contrasts and gentle, harmonious tones.

When buying bedroom furniture, there are plenty of beds to pick from, including wrought-iron cribs, old hospital beds, and bassinets. If you are buying a crib or bassinet for a young baby, it is advisable to buy a new mattress for reasons of good hygiene.

Scour markets for small chests of drawers; if you find a painted chest, you can always strip it and repaint it in your child's favorite color. Children who can dress themselves will love having storage that is easy to access, so put their clothes in big

ABOVE **If you find an old armchair in reasonable condition, customize it for a children's bedroom by re-upholstering it in colorful thick fabrics or sewing a slipcover. Take home waifs and strays such as this floppy-eared bunny.**

THIS PAGE Create a patchwork of patterns on a bed. Here striped pillow cases, floral pillow covers, and chinoiserie-style sheets come together to make an eye-catching mélange.

OPPOSITE Vibrant eye-candy for a little girl, the wall behind the armoire is a collage of wallpaper scraps, collected from ends of rolls, pattern books, and swatch samples.

colored shopping baskets or sturdy cardboard boxes covered in wallpaper remnants or gift wrap. A small reclaimed armoire is always useful, but if your child likes choosing his or her own clothes, you could string up a clothesline or fasten a pole between two solid wooden posts nailed to the wall to make a small-scale open closet.

For bedroom chairs, reupholster or create covers for secondhand armchairs from colorful, sturdy vintage-textile finds such as canvas, ticking fabrics, former curtains, and bedspreads. Or accessorize a plain armchair with brightly colored cushion covers adapted from vintage fabrics such as old scarves, aprons, and dresses.

Cover your child's bed in colorful finds such as crocheted blanket or patchwork quilts, or dye plain baby blankets. Making a patchwork bedcover for an adult's bed is daunting, but creating a patchwork throw from vintage finds for a baby's crib is less of a challenge; you can always add bits as your baby moves from bassinet to crib to single bed. Old children's clothes, particularly those incorporating bits of embroidery, lacework, or prints, are an ideal starting point for a patchwork cover. One natural

LEFT **Hand-me-downs like these children's chairs often end up in markets when they get to the end of the line; in this case, all that was needed was a new coat of paint. Children like things with a sense of fun, such as the blow-up beach balls and globes hung from the ceiling. Look for mural-sized artworks like this Russian scene, which absorbs children for hours.**

RIGHT **Take some of the work out of homework by giving your children a bright and sunny place to study. In this room, a 1970s-style storage system is used to clear away pens, pencils, rulers, and other stationery. For a study light, a rusty gooseneck lamp has been sprayed with cherry-red gloss paint, and an old typist's chair has been repainted butter yellow.**

Children love bright color schemes, but temper loud colors with deep contrasts and gentle, harmonious tones.

fabric that is kind and gentle on young children's skin is linen. If you find antique linen sheets, simply cut them up to crib sizes and dye them.

Good storage in children's bedrooms is essential, especially if your child is a natural magpie. Most children also like to see their belongings, so try to mix open storage with chests, boxes, or suitcases. For open shelving, reuse old bookshelves.

No matter how hard you try to resist, you will find that you often go to a market with your own must-get shopping list and return with a collection of orphaned toys. Secondhand finds usually cost half the amount of new ones and, given the

fickleness of children's affections, buying from markets means that you won't have spent a fortune on something that is loved only for five minutes.

While markets offer plenty of yesterday's toys—old tin soldiers, stuffed animals, rocking horses, and Russian dolls—you will also find a huge array of grown-up playthings and knickknacks that children adore: old trinket boxes, perfume bottles, garden gnomes, seashells, cowboy hats, garlands—you name it. If you are brave, take your child along with you to a secondhand market and see it from their perspective. If you get them to enjoy shopping from markets at an early age, they'll love it for life.

THIS PAGE **Instead of a conventional chest of drawers, reclaim an old desk and paint it a vibrant color. The beautiful old Danish wooden crib is clothed in vintage fabric pillows and patchwork and woolen blankets.**

LEFT Former industrial pieces—such as the low-hanging factory lights, the long factory table (with its gorgeous customized legs) and the wall of paper-filing cabinets—suit a former industrial space. Around the table is a collection of ex-office seats and factory chairs with swivel bases.

While some simply need a space to study, write letters, and pay bills, for more and more of us the home office is our workplace.

work spaces

Tailor-made secondhand items for work spaces at home generally come from their original habitats: offices. Some pieces do turn up at markets, but office liquidation sales, office furniture auctions, and secondhand office furniture outlets are often more fruitful picking grounds.

Office desks, available in various configurations, are ideal for the job for which they were designed. If a desk is too corporate in appearance, replace its pinstriped suit with a colorful coat of paint or hide it under an old tablecloth. If the desk has drawers, consider painting each drawer a different color or giving the drawers a new set of knobs.

Early examples of desks, such as large rolltop desks, often come with plenty of built-in storage. Sometimes "working" tables, built for long hours of labour—architects' drawing boards, leather-and-fabric cutting tables, factory assembly tables, and antique sewing-machine trestles (*sans* machine)—turn up at markets when warehouses are stripped out, but tables that are more commonly found, such as old school desks, small pine dining tables, and glass-topped tables, work equally well.

Another solution is to make your own. For a cheap chic desk, rest a plain door on two support pillars such as towers of bricks, wooden trestles, bedside chests, or a duo of filing cabinets.

A good chair is essential. If you will be spending a lot of time at your desk, choose one that provides adequate support. Try your chair before you buy it and remember the rules: your feet should be firmly planted on the floor (if they don't reach the floor, a foot-rest of secondhand books or an old winebox will do); your lower back must be well supported; and your arms must be at right angles to the top of the desk. Consider acquiring a typist's chair, which will be fully adjustable and ergonomically designed to support your posture. Give your chair a new personality by reupholstering the seat and backrest in funky vintage-fabric finds.

Other chairs, such as leather boardroom chairs, architects' stools, school chairs, and simple wooden

RIGHT Metal cabinets can be easily painted or stripped, but an original color like this looks just right in this industrial-style room with its backdrop of painted brickwork. Pens, rulers, and paintbrushes are stored on top of the cabinet in vases, tin cups, old mugs, and bottles.

THIS PAGE There are all sorts of ways to fashion a desk. Here, old wooden trestles are crowned with a shiny new reinforced-glass top. A folded blanket is used instead of cushions to soften the seat of the chair. The table lamp, with its odd pairing of long, elegant base and frumpy shade, looks eccentric.

THIS PAGE Industrial-look finds are brought together here to create a hard-working work station. Factory discoveries such as the desk, chair, and metal shelving unit sometimes surface at markets. On the desk is the perfect personal lighting assistant: a draftsman's lamp.

chairs will also serve your desk well. If you need to adjust a chair to your height, shorten its legs with a saw or put a cushion on the seat.

Every work space needs a light designed with reading in mind, and there is nothing to beat the adjustable gooseneck desk light (but check the joints and springs to make sure they are not too stiff or saggy). Small bedside reading lamps or large floor lamps also throw out plenty of light.

In addition to office storage, most of us require some kind of filing system for keeping our personal papers in order. Office furniture will do the job well, but may need customizing to fit in with a particular room's décor. Other storage ideas include old mailroom shelves, chests of drawers, old metal gym lockers, old bookshelves, doorless armoires and, for files, plate racks nailed to walls.

To keep your desk neat, unearth something to suit your secondhand style rather than the usual plastic desk caddy more commonly spotted in low-ceilinged offices with gray walls. Store your pens,

OPPOSITE PAGE This work corner, sectioned off with a patchwork of silk scarves, is home to a rolltop desk, complete with its own storage.

LEFT You can find a work niche like this one in "dead" space beside the stairs. An industrial light is attached to the side of the staircase, lighting a former printing-factory desk.

ABOVE This tiny work space is shoehorned into a living-room corner. An ex-mailroom cabinet gives lots of storage for paperwork.

pencils, rulers, and scissors in vintage vases, milk jugs, old tins, tea caddies, jelly jars—whatever you can find. Builders' plastic odds-'n'-ends boxes—which are normally reserved for housing nails and screws—are ideal for staples, paperclips, erasers, and pencil sharpeners.

Markets often reveal other early examples of desk accessories, including old Bakelite phones, quills and inkpots, kitsch paperweights, antique typewriters, and bone-handled paper knives.

For storing notepads, staplers, hole-punchers, and CDs, buy larger containers such as antique leather suitcases, jewelry chests, and hatboxes or cardboard shoeboxes jazzed up with vintage wallpaper or wrapping paper.

resources

For listings of flea markets held throughout the country, go to www.fleausa.com, www.fleamarketguide.com, or wee.fleamarket.com. For inspiration, visit www.carterjunk.com, a site for the true flea-market devotee. When traveling, call the area Chamber of Commerce for information about local flea markets.

Aloha Flea Market
9500 Salt Lake Boulevard
(in the parking lot of Aloha Stadium)
Honolulu, HA
tel: 808-730-9611
Held every Wednesday, Saturday, and Sunday. For more than 20 years, this outdoor market has catered to the eclectic tastes of America's westernmost residents.

All-American Trade Day
11190 U.S. Highway 413
(between Albertville and Gunterville)
Gunterville, AL
tel: 205-891-2790
Held weekends all year. In addition to collectibles, this indoor and outdoor market sells livestock, poultry, and fresh produce.

American Park'n'Swap
40th Street and Washington Street
Phoenix, AZ
tel: 602-273-1258
www.americanparknswap.com
Held every Wednesday evening, Friday, Saturday, and Sunday.

Anderson Jockey Lot and Farmer's Market
Highway 29 North
Belton, SC
tel: 864-224-2027
Every weekend, 1,500 to 2,000 vendors spread their wares over 65 acres.

The Annex Antiques Fair and Flea Market
Sixth Avenue from 24th to 27th Streets
New York, NY
tel: 212-243-5343
Two work-a-day parking lots turn into flea markets every Saturday and Sunday all year. Other lots, indoors and out, have joined the bandwagon and the whole area blossoms with vintage and antique stuff on weekends.

Brimfield Antiques and Collectibles
Route 20
Brimfield, MA
tel: 413-245-3436
www.brimfieldshow.com
Held first week of May, July, and September. Dealers come from all over—including Europe—bringing everything from large pieces of furniture to silver to vintage linens.

Broadacres Swap Meet
2930 Las Vegas Boulevard North
(at Pecos Street)
North Las Vegas, NV
tel: 702-642-3777
www.broadacresswapmeet.com
Held every Friday, Saturday, and Sunday all year, this outdoor flea market is the oldest and largest in Nevada. Look for "treasures" that have relocated to the Southwest with their owners as well as local items.

Englishtown Auction Sales
90 Wilson Avenue
Englishtown, NJ
tel: 732-446-9644
Held every Saturday and Sunday all year. Also open on special holidays and the five days before Christmas. In operation since the 1920s and covering over 100 acres, indoors and out, you'll find items from professional dealers as well as one-time attic clearers.

The Colorado Springs Flea Market
5225 East Platte Avenue
(Highway 24)
Colarado Springs, CO
tel: 719-380-8599
www.csfleamarket.com
Held every Saturday and Sunday all year, as well as Fridays from June through September. This outdoor market has the tang of the Old West.

Flea Market at Eastern Market
Seventh Street, SE at Eastern Market
(half block from Pennsylvania Avenue on Capitol Hill)
Washington, DC
tel: 703-534-7612
www.easternmarket.net
Held Sundays from March through Christmas. This 15-year-old flea market has a real old-fashioned neighborhood charm along with the international atmosphere the area provides.

Fort Lauderdale Swap Shop
3291 W. Sunrise Boulevard
Fort Lauderdale, FL
tel: 954-791-7927
Held every day of the year from 6 a.m. to 6 p.m. Professional dealers and locals exhibit a wide variety of "stuff."

French Market: Community Flea Market
1235 North Peters Street (Elysian Fields at the Mississippi River)
New Orleans, LA
tel: 504-596-3420
Held daily out-of-doors, weather permitting. In place since the 18th century, this market represents New Orlean's fancy but faded decorating style. It's near many of the attractions of this cosmopolitan city.

Hartville Marketplace and Flea Market
1289 Edison Street NW
Hartville, OH
tel: 330-877-9860
www.hartvillefleamarket.com
Held Mondays, Thursdays, and Saturdays, April. Look for the Amish and Mennonite food purveyors as well as dealers in all sorts of merchandise. This flea market has a real country flavor.

Hinckley Flea Market
803 Highway 48 at I-35 (look for five large red-and-white buildings)
Hinckley, MN
tel: 320-384-9911
Operates weekly from May to September, Thursdays through Sunday. This is Minnesota's most modern market. You'll find camp-grounds as well as collectibles, and there's a casino nearby.

Jack Loeks' Flea Market
1400 28th Street SW (three miles west of Route 131, in the Studio 28 parking lot)
Grand Rapids, MI
tel: 616-532-8218
Held every weekend from April through October, rain or shine. For 30 years this outdoor antiques and collectibles flea market has been selling all sorts of attic treasures and soon-to-be collectibles.

Kane County Flea Market
Rt. 64 and Randall Road
St. Charles, IL
tel: 630-377-2252
www.kanecountyfleamarket.com
Held every second Sunday, from May through October. Indoor and outdoor booths specializing in heartland antiques and collectibles.

Lakewood Antiques Market
2000 Lakewood Way
Atlanta. GA
tel: 404-622-4488
www.lakewoodantiques.com
Held every Friday, Saturday, and Sunday on the second full weekend of each month. Antiques, collectibles, and rediscovered treasures are the only things featured here.

Long Beach Outdoor Antiques and Collectibles Market
Veteran Boulevard at Lakewood Boulevard
Long Beach, CA
tel: 213-655-5703
www.longbeachantiquemarket.com
Held the third Sunday of every month. A wide variety of merchandise from regular dealers as well as private individuals.

Mary's Ole TIme Swap Meet
7925 Northeast 23rd Street
Oklahoma City, OK
tel: 405-427-0051
Held every weekend year-round. For over 30 years people have been shopping at Mary's, indoors and out.

Metrolina Expo
7100 North Statesville Road (off I-77)
Charlotte, NC
tel: 800-824-3770
www.metrolineaexpotradeshow.com
Held every Friday through Sunday year-round. For nearly three decades, this has been the area's place to search for collectibles and vintage items. Special emphasis on antiques the first weekend of each month.

Picc-a-dilly Flea Market
796 West 13th Street
(Lane County Fairgrounds)
Eugene, OR
tel: 541-683-5589
Held the 1st and 3rd Sundays of every month. Call to verify specific dates. Since 1970 this flea market has attracted dealers from all over, selling a wide variety of antiques and collectibles.

Redwood Swap Meet
3688 Redwood Road
Salt Lake City, UT
tel: 801-973-6060
Held every Saturday and Sunday, weather permitting. This market offers a wide variety of collectibles and vintage items.

Renningers Market
740 Noble Street
Kutztown, PA
tel: 717-385-0104
www.renningers.com
Held every Friday and Saturday year-round. "Extravaganzas" are held on Saturday and Sunday in late April, late June, and late September. Call for dates. Amish, Pennsylvania Dutch, primitive, and folk art are the specialties at this long-standing and well-known flea market, but you'll find lots of everything.

The Rose Bowl Flea Market
Pasadena, CA
tel: 626-588-4411
Held the second Sunday of every month. Vintage goods from high kitsch to fine furnishings.

Anchorage Market and Festival
Third and E Streets (across from the Hilton Hotel)
Anchorage, Alaska
tel: 907-276-7207
www.anchoragemarkets.com
Held every Sunday from mid-May through mid-September. In addition to antiques and collectibles, new merchandise and crafts are featured as well as fresh produce in season.

Tennessee State Fairgrounds Flea Market
Wedgewood Avenue and Nolensville Road (State Fairgrounds)
Nashville, TN
tel: 615-862-5016
Held the fourth weekend of every month, except December, when the maket is held on the third weekend. This long-standing flea market is a Nashville tradition, playing host to almost 1,200 vendors.

Traders Village
7979 North Eldridge Parkway
Houston, TX
tel: 281-890-5500
www.tradersvillage.com
Held every weekend year-round. With a keen understanding of the needs of collectors, this market has, in addition to acres of "stuff," rides for the kids, cash machines, and a park for recreational vehicles.

picture credits

All photography by Debi Treloar.

key **a**=above, **b**=below, **r**=right, **l**=left, **c**=center.

Endpapers Story; **page 1** designer Petra Boase & family's home in Norfolk; **2** designer Susanne Rutzou's home in Copenhagen; **3** Debi Treloar's home in London; **4** Sigolène Prébois of Tsé &Tsé associées home in Paris; **5** Catherine Lévy of Tsé &Tsé associées home in Paris; **12–13** author, stylist and Caravan (store) owner Emily Chalmers and director Chris Richmond's home in London; **14** owner of Crème de la Crème à la Edgar, Helle Høgsbro Krag's home in Copenhagen; **15 inset** Debi Treloar's home in London; **16a** owners of Maisonette, Martin Barrell & Amanda Sellers' home in London; **16bl** Debi Treloar's home in London; **16br** the home in Copenhagen of producer Samina Langholz of Bullet Productions (www.bullet.dk); **17** Debi Treloar's home in London; **18** & **19r** owners of Maisonette, Martin Barrell & Amanda Sellers' home in London; **19l** designer Susanne Rutzou's home in Copenhagen; **20a** Sigolène Prébois of Tsé &Tsé associées home in Paris; **20b** the Philadelphia home of Glen Senk & Keith Johnson of Anthropologie; **21** Anita Calero; **22–23** designer Susanne Rutzou's home in Copenhagen; **24al** the Philadelphia home of Kristin Norris, creative director at Anthropologie, and Trevor Lunn, digital designer; **24bl** Catherine Lévy of Tsé &Tsé associées home in Paris; **24r** & **25** owner of Crème de la Crème à la Edgar, Helle Høgsbro Krag's home in Copenhagen; **26** Debi Treloar's home in London; **27 background** the Chestnut Hill home of Pamela Falk; **27 inset** designer Petra Boase & family's home in Norfolk; **28** owners of Maisonette, Martin Barrell & Amanda Sellers' home in London; **28 inset** Debi Treloar's home in London; **29, 30** & **31l** author, stylist and Caravan (store) owner Emily Chalmers and director Chris Richmond's home in London; **31r** Debi Treloar's home in London; **32al** designer Susanne Rutzou's home in Copenhagen; **32ar** the Philadelphia home of Kristin Norris, creative director at Anthropologie, and Trevor Lunn, digital designer; **32b** the Philadelphia home of Glen Senk & Keith Johnson of Anthropologie; **33l** designer Susanne Rutzou's home in Copenhagen; **33r** Story; **34 both** designer Petra Boase & family's home in Norfolk; **35–36** Debi Treloar's home in London; **37l** the home in Copenhagen of producer Samina Langholz of Bullet Productions (www.bullet.dk); **37r both** designer Petra Boase & family's home in Norfolk; **38–39** designer Susanne Rutzou's home in Copenhagen; **39bl** the Philadelphia home of Glen Senk & Keith Johnson of Anthropologie; **39ar** the home in Copenhagen of producer Samina Langholz of Bullet Productions (www.bullet.dk); **40** the guesthouse of the interior designer & artist Philippe Guilmin, Brussels; **40 inset** & **41** owner of Crème de la Crème à la Edgar, Helle Høgsbro Krag's home in Copenhagen; **42** the home in Copenhagen of producer Samina Langholz of Bullet Productions (www.bullet.dk); **43** the guesthouse of the interior designer & artist Philippe Guilmin, Brussels; **44** owners of Maisonette, Martin Barrell & Amanda Sellers' home in London; **45bl**&**ar** designer Susanne Rutzou's home in Copenhagen; **45c** owner of Crème de la Crème à la Edgar, Helle Høgsbro Krag's home in Copenhagen; **46** the home in Copenhagen of producer Samina Langholz of Bullet Productions (www.bullet.dk); **47bl** designer Susanne Rutzou's home in Copenhagen; **47ar** owner of Crème de la Crème à la Edgar, Helle Høgsbro Krag's home in Copenhagen; **48al** the home in Copenhagen of producer Samina Langholz of Bullet Productions (www.bullet.dk); **48bl, 48ar** & **49** the guesthouse of the interior designer & artist Philippe Guilmin, Brussels; **50** author, stylist and Caravan (store) owner Emily Chalmers and director Chris Richmond's home in London; **51l** Debi Treloar's home in London; **51r both** Catherine Lévy of Tsé &Tsé associées home in Paris; **52** the Chestnut Hill home of Pamela Falk; **53 inset** the Chestnut Hill home of Pamela Falk; **54** the guesthouse of the interior designer & artist Philippe Guilmin, Brussels; **55 main** the guesthouse of the interior designer & artist Philippe Guilmin, Brussels; **55 inset** designer Steven Shailer's apartment in New York City; **56 main** Catherine Lévy of Tsé &Tsé associées home in Paris; **56 inset** designer Petra Boase & family's home in Norfolk; **57l** Debi Treloar's home in London; **57r** the home in Copenhagen of producer Samina Langholz of Bullet Productions (www.bullet.dk); **58l** owners of Maisonette, Martin Barrell & Amanda Sellers' home in London; **58r** Debi Treloar's home in London; **59** Sigolène Prébois of Tsé &Tsé associées home in Paris; **60** John Derian's apartment in New York; **61c** Anita Calero; **61bl** Catherine Lévy of Tsé &Tsé associées home in Paris; **61br** the home in Copenhagen of producer Samina Langholz of Bullet Productions (www.bullet.dk); **62al** the Philadelphia home of Glen Senk & Keith Johnson of Anthropologie; **62bl** owner of Crème de la Crème à la Edgar, Helle Høgsbro Krag's home in Copenhagen; **62ar** John Derian's apartment in New York; **62br** the Chestnut Hill home of Pamela Falk; **63l** the Philadelphia home of Glen Senk & Keith Johnson of Anthropologie; **63r** designer Steven Shailer's apartment in New York City; **64 all** designer Susanne Rutzou's home in Copenhagen; **65 inset** Anita Calero; **65 main** designer Susanne Rutzou's home in Copenhagen; **66al** & **bc** Catherine Lévy of Tsé &Tsé associées home in Paris; **66ar** & **67** author, stylist and Caravan (store) owner Emily Chalmers and director Chris Richmond's home in London; **68–69** all Story except **68ar inset** owners of Maisonette, Martin Barrell & Amanda Sellers' home in London; **70–71 all** Catherine Lévy of Tsé &Tsé associées home in Paris except **70ar** the Philadelphia home of Kristin Norris, creative director at Anthropologie, and Trevor Lunn, digital designer; **72–73** the home in Copenhagen of producer Samina Langholz of Bullet Productions (www.bullet.dk); **74–75** author, stylist and Caravan (store) owner Emily Chalmers and director Chris Richmond's home in London; **76–77** the home in Copenhagen of producer Samina Langholz of Bullet Productions (www.bullet.dk); **78** designer Susanne Rutzou's home in Copenhagen; **79** owners of Maisonette, Martin Barrell & Amanda Sellers' home in London; **80** the guesthouse of the interior designer & artist Philippe Guilmin, Brussels; **81** owner of Crème de la Crème à la Edgar, Helle Høgsbro Krag's home in Copenhagen; **82b** John Derian's apartment in New York; **82a** designer Steven Shailer's apartment in New York City; **83** Anita Calero; **84** the Philadelphia home of Glen Senk & Keith Johnson of Anthropologie; **85** the Philadelphia home of Kristin Norris, creative director at Anthropologie, and Trevor Lunn, digital designer; **86** Story; **87** Debi Treloar's home in London; **88–89** Catherine Lévy of Tsé &Tsé associées home in Paris; **90–91** the guesthouse of the interior designer & artist Philippe Guilmin, Brussels; **92** the Philadelphia home of Kristin Norris, creative director at Anthropologie, and Trevor Lunn, digital designer; **93 all** Sigolène Prébois of Tsé &Tsé associées home in Paris; **94–95** owners of Maisonette, Martin Barrell & Amanda Sellers' home in London; **96–97** Debi Treloar's home in London; **98** John Derian's apartment in New York; **98–99** author, stylist and Caravan (store) owner Emily Chalmers and director Chris Richmond's home in London; **99** owner of Crème de la Crème à la Edgar, Helle Høgsbro Krag's home in Copenhagen; **100–101 all** Story; **102–103** designer Susanne Rutzou's home in Copenhagen; **104l** the Philadelphia home of Glen Senk & Keith Johnson of Anthropologie; **104–105** the Chestnut Hill home of Pamela Falk; **105** John Derian's apartment in New York; **106–107** Catherine Lévy of Tsé &Tsé associées home in Paris; **108–109** owners of Maisonette, Martin Barrell & Amanda Sellers' home in London; **110** owner of Crème de la Crème à la Edgar, Helle Høgsbro Krag's home in Copenhagen; **111** the guesthouse of the interior designer & artist Philippe Guilmin, Brussels; **112** designer Petra Boase & family's home in Norfolk; **113** author, stylist and Caravan (store) owner Emily Chalmers and director Chris Richmond's home in London; **114r** the home in Copenhagen of producer Samina Langholz of Bullet Productions (www.bullet.dk); **114l, 115** & **116** Debi Treloar's home in London; **117–19** designer Petra Boase & family's home in Norfolk; **120** & **121r** author, stylist and Caravan (store) owner Emily Chalmers and director Chris Richmond's home in London; **121l** Sigolène Prébois of Tsé &Tsé associées home in Paris; **122** the guesthouse of the interior designer & artist Philippe Guilmin, Brussels; **123** Story; **124–25** the guesthouse of the interior designer & artist Philippe Guilmin, Brussels; **126** Sigolène Prébois of Tsé &Tsé associées home in Paris; **127** designer Petra Boase & family's home in Norfolk; **128–29** Debi Treloar's home in London; **130** Sigolène Prébois of Tsé &Tsé associées home in Paris; **131–33** owner of Crème de la Crème à la Edgar, Helle Høgsbro Krag's home in Copenhagen; **134–35** the guesthouse of the interior designer & artist Philippe Guilmin, Brussels; **136** John Derian's apartment in New York; **137** the Philadelphia home of Glen Senk & Keith Johnson of Anthropologie; **138** author, stylist and Caravan (store) owner Emily Chalmers and director Chris Richmond's home in London; **139b** Sigolène Prébois of Tsé &Tsé associées home in Paris; **139a** designer Steven Shailer's apartment in New York City.

business credits

Anita Calero Photography

521 West 23rd Street # 6R
New York, NY 10011
212-727-8949

www.apostrophe.net

Pages 21, 61c, 65 inset, 83.

Anthropologie

800-309-2500

www.anthropologie.com

*Pages 20b, 24al, 32ar, 32b, 39bl, 62al, 63l,
70ar, 84, 85, 92, 104l, 137.*

Bois-Renard

Decorative home accessories
215-247-4777

*Pages 27 background, 52, 53 inset, 62br,
104–105.*

Bullet Productions

www.bullet.dk

*Pages 16br, 37l, 39ar, 42, 46, 48al, 57r, 61br,
72–73, 76–77, 114r.*

Crème de la Crème à la Edgar

Kompagnistræde 8,st
1208 Copenhagen K
Denmark
+ 45-33361818

www.cremedelacremealaedgar.dk

*Pages 14, 24r, 25, 40 inset, 41 , 45c, 47ar, 62bl,
81, 99, 110, 131–33.*

Debi Treloar

www.debitreloar.com

*Pages 3, 15 inset, 16bl, 17, 26, 28 inset, 31r,
35–36, 51l, 57l, 58r, 87, 96–97, 114l, 115,
116, 128–29.*

Emily Chalmers

author & stylist

www.emilychalmers.com

Caravan
11 Lamb Street
Spitalfields
London E1 6EA
UK
+ 44-(0)20-7247-6467

www.caravanstyle.com

*Pages 12–13, 29, 30, 31l, 50, 66ar, 67, 74–75,
98–99, 113, 120, 121r, 138.*

John Derian

store
6 East 2nd Street
New York, NY 10003
212-677-3917

www.johnderian.com

Pages 60, 62ar, 82b, 98, 105, 136

Maisonette

+ 44-(0)20-8964-8444

maisonette.uk@aol.com
www.maisonette.uk.com
For location booking, please call Richard
Smith at InSpace 07050 189 375.

*Pages 16a, 18, 19r, 28, 44, 58l, 68ar, 79,
94–95, 108–109.*

Petra Boase

www.petraboaseshop.com
info@petraboase.com

*Pages 1, 27 inset, 34 both, 37r, 56 inset, 112,
117–19, 127.*

Philippe Guilmin

interior designer & artist

philippe.guilmin@skynet.be

*Pages 40, 43, 48bl, 48ar, 49, 54, 55 main, 80,
90–91, 111, 122, 124–25, 134–35.*

Rützou A/S

+ 45-35240616

www.rutzou.com
cph@rutzou.com

*Pages 2, 19l, 22–23, 32al, 33l, 38–39, 45bl,
45ar, 47bl, 64, 65 main, 78, 103.*

Steven Shailer

917-518-8001

Pages 55 inset, 63r, 82a, 139a.

Story

4 Wilkes Street
London E1 6QF
UK
+ 44-(0)20-7377-0313
Story is an ever-changing & evolving lifestyle
gallery/shop located near Brick Lane market.
Part of the Story project is 'Story Deli'—a
must for East End visitors.

*Endpapers, pages 33r, 68–69 (all except 68ar),
86, 100–101, 123.*

Tsé & Tsé associées

Catherine Lévy & Sigolène Prébois

www.tse-tse.com

*Pages 4, 5, 20a, 24bl, 51r, 56 main, 59, 61bl,
66al, 66bc, 70–71, 88–89, 93, 106–107, 121l,
126, 130, 139b.*

index

Page numbers in *italics* refer to illustrations.

acknowledgments

Emily Chalmers would like to thank everyone who made this book possible, especially Alison Starling, for dreaming up the wonderful project; Gabriella Le Grazie, for getting in touch and directing us in her special way; Emily Westlake, for her support; Paul Tilby, for his graphics skills; and Henrietta Heald and all the hard-working team at Ryland Peters & Small. Ali, thank you once again for your optimism and inspiration; and thank you to all those flea-market fans who allowed us to feature their wonderful homes.

A special thank you goes to the lovely Debi Treloar—my flea-market friend.

Ali Hanan's thanks goes to Henrietta Heald for her thoughtful, sensitive editing; to Alison Starling for asking her to work on such a lovely book; to the vivacious, warm, and wonderful Emily Chalmers for her flowers, conversation, and inspirational ideas; and to her own in-house team, Dizzy, Luca, and tiny Rosa.